BURMA

Travelling through thousands of miles of Burmese landscape, the author captured the essence of this country before the internal political problems broke. Filled with lively descriptions of Burma - from its bustling cities to its lush jungles - the highlight of the book is the author's story of his long journey up the Irrawaddy River. Supplemented by the author's own illustrations, this book conveys Kelly's appreciation of the beauty of the country and the happiness of its people.

BURMA

R. TALBOT KELLY

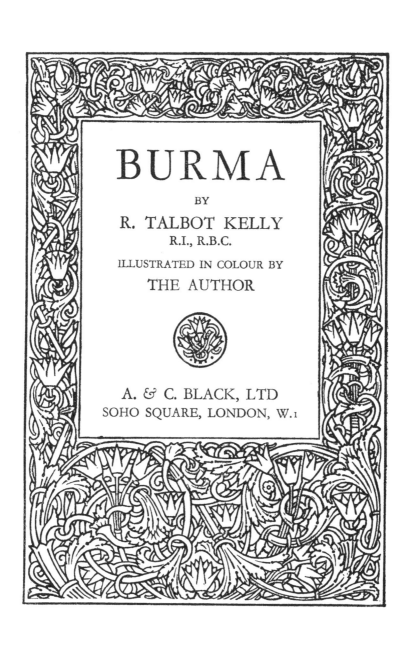

BURMA

BY

R. TALBOT KELLY
R.I., R.B.C.

ILLUSTRATED IN COLOUR BY

THE AUTHOR

A. & C. BLACK, LTD
SOHO SQUARE, LONDON, W.1

Originally published in 1933 by A&C Black.

First published in 2004 by Kegan Paul.

This edition first published in 2009 by
Routledge
2 Park Square, Milton Park, Abingdon, Oxon, OX14 4RN

Simultaneously published in the USA and Canada
by Routledge
711 Third Avenue, New York, NY 10017

Routledge is an imprint of the Taylor & Francis Group, an informa business

First issued in paperback 2012

British Library Cataloguing in Publication Data
A catalogue record for this book is available from the British Library

ISBN 13: 9780710309716 (hbk)
ISBN 13: 9780415540988 (pbk)

Publisher's Note
The publisher has gone to great lengths to ensure the quality of this reprint
but points out that some imperfections in the original copies may be
apparent. The publisher has made every effort to contact original copyright
holders and would welcome correspondence from those they have been
unable to trace.

TO
MY FATHER AND MOTHER

Preface to the Second Edition

THE demand for a new edition of this book reflects the increased public interest in Burma, largely due to recent internal problems and her relation to India and the Empire. This volume, however, does not concern itself with political questions but is frankly a narrative of incidents and impressions experienced in my seven months' sojourn there, now twenty-eight years ago. As a personal record of first impressions of the scenery and life of the country, therefore, it still holds good in main essentials, and in this new edition I have merely made a few minor alterations and explanatory footnotes which the lapse of time has made desirable.

In my journeyings of some 3500 miles in Burma I enjoyed throughout the proverbial hospitality of the East, and though many of my kind hosts have passed away, and the heads of the great corporations who so greatly assisted me in my work have gone into honourable retirement, I must ever hold them in most grateful remembrance.

Burma

Inevitably I was able to touch only the fringe of the immensity of subjects contained in Burma's 156,000 square miles of tropical beauty. The difficulties, more- over, under which I worked were great : arduous journeys through forest and jungle, climatic conditions most unkind to the painter, difficulties of language and of health. What I saw and experienced in Burma was, however, in the main typical of the country as a whole, and has left a lasting impression on my mind, and I am not without the hope that this book, im- perfect as it is, may succeed in conveying some truthful impression of the beauty of the country, some little insight into the happy picturesqueness of its people, and may perhaps excite in some of my readers the desire to see and study the country for themselves.

R. T. K.

1932

Contents

CHAPTER I

Burma

CHAPTER VII

Illustrations

Sketch-map of Burma on page xii

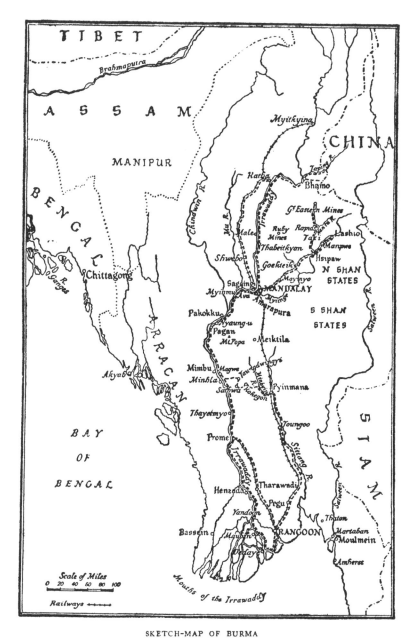

SKETCH-MAP OF BURMA

The dotted line indicates the Author's route

BURMA

CHAPTER I

RANGOON

OUR pleasant voyage was drawing to its close, and there was not one of the passengers of the Bibby liner by which I was travelling but experienced a feeling akin to home-sickness as the time approached for us to bid farewell to the s.s. *Yorkshire*, now within a few hours of arriving at Rangoon.

The final match at skittles had been played on the spacious fore-deck, followed by the last of many concerts which, with dances, had from time to time been arranged in order to relieve the "monotony" of a voyage that had not known a tedious moment. Our run out had been uneventfully happy, and the weather perfect.

The last few days' journey, across the Indian Ocean, accorded well with the spirit of content which pervaded the ship, as, the temperature pleasantly modified

Burma

by monsoon showers, we would watch the shoals of bonito-driven flying-fish skim its oily undulations, and admire the stately frigate-birds which soared overhead or, regardless of the speedy leviathan which so closely passed them, rested peacefully upon the smooth surface of the ocean.

Yet it was a strange land we were approaching that October morning, and regrets gave place to anticipation as, awaiting our summons from the "bath-wallah," we lounged about the after-deck in the early dawn and looked for the first appearance of the land. Few of us except the Anglo-Burmans on board had any knowledge of the country we were about to visit, and all looked forward to pleasurable surprises in store with an eagerness hardly tempered by the apprehension of snakes or malaria, which many smoke-room "yarns" told on the voyage might well have engendered.

It must be confessed, however, that my first view of Burma in the grey dawn was distinctly disappointing.

The low alluvial mud banks, scarcely raised above high-water mark, and covered with scrub jungle and "kaing" grass, were certainly not inviting, though those who knew could tell tales of tiger and other large game in these wastes, and of a picturesque life hidden away among the palm groves which dotted the plains.

Entering the river, the turbid waters of the Irrawaddy presented little of interest save a stray catamaran or unlovely Chinese "paddy" boat, and even the picturesquely named "Elephant Point" and "Monkey Point" conveyed little to the new arrival.

Rangoon

Proceeding upstream, however, new growths aroused our interest—cocoa-nut and toddy palms, tamarinds and mangoes, among which the trimly thatched huts of the Burmans or an occasional pagoda furnished the necessary touch of local colour. Nevertheless the scene was tame, and to myself at least disappointing, until, after a couple of hours' steaming, there suddenly appeared, rosy in the sunshine, the golden dome of the great Shwe Dagon Pagoda, seemingly suspended above the purple haze which still hid Rangoon from sight.

From this moment everything appeared changed, and the freed imagination found possibilities everywhere. Numerous creeks enter the Rangoon river, leading to regions unexplored and mysterious ; from them emerge into the main stream the quaintly shaped boats of the Burmans—strange craft, whose graceful lines and richly carved sterns seem to reflect the minds of a people who love beauty and are content to be happy.

Increasing numbers of steam launches, "paddy"[1] boats, and sampans marked our nearer approach to Rangoon, and imaginings gave place to more practical thoughts as the steamer came to an anchor and we prepared to land.

The decks were soon crowded. Native porters, personal servants of returning "Sahibs," or Eurasian officials, took possession of the steamer and incidentally of anything visible that might perchance be legally claimed as a possible possession of their employers. I must, however, express some surprise at the action of the

[1] Unhusked rice.

Burma

Customs. Everything in the shape of firearms was at once seized and placed in bond, and in view of the still occasional cases of dacoity such precautions (especially in the case of the .303 rifle) are intelligible and justified ; but why should such palpably innocent impedimenta as "kodaks" or field-glasses come under the same embargo ? True, all such belongings were quickly and politely returned at the custom-house in exchange for a simple form of declaration ; but it struck me as a somewhat unnecessary and irritating formality, especially to a new arrival all uncertain of his bearings or how to go about things. Otherwise the Customs are easy, and in all cases their officials were polite, even assiduous, in their well-meant attentions.

Half-an-hour after landing found me very comfortably installed in the Strand Hotel, a roomy bedroom with bathroom attached having been allotted to me, while its large enclosed verandah, which practically formed a sitting-room, gave me ample breathing space ; and, making allowance for the latitude, the table-d'hôte was excellent and varied. I was a little disconcerted, however, the first night on retiring, to find that my bed was furnished with mattrass, pillow, and mosquito-net only, no sheet or covering of any kind being provided. I imagined this to be an oversight; but the omission soon explained itself when I found that the thermometer never dropped below ninety-eight degrees all night, and in the damp heat that prevailed it would have been impossible to have endured the weight of even a silk coverlet.

THE PAGODA STEPS, RANGOON

Rangoon

The morning after my arrival I was able to engage a native (Indian) servant, by name Chinnasammy, an excellent " boy " of forty or so, who had served through the Burma war of '87 as officer's and mess servant, and who was afterwards to prove of the greatest service to me, as he spoke English and a little Burmese, while I was entirely ignorant of the latter language; and, quite apart from his services as " bearer," it would have been almost impossible for me, or any one ignorant of Burmese, to have travelled through the country in comfort without the assistance of an interpreter. Even in Rangoon itself, Europeanised though it is, English alone is a broken reed upon which to rely where half the languages of the Asiatic world are spoken, and hardly one of the Eastern races represented has any knowledge of a Western tongue.

Rangoon is interesting—palpably a prosperous and in some ways a handsome city, and is a perfect kaleidoscope of human life.

Built upon the east bank of the river, 30 miles from the sea, it covers an area of 15 square miles, its frontage to the river consisting of excellent quays and " godowns "[1] behind which lies the commercial town. The river runs by in deeply swirling eddies, dangerous to life should you accidentally find yourself in the water.

Moored to the wharves, or anchored in midstream, are a surprisingly large number of ocean steamers; prominent among them are the magnificent steamers of the Bibby line, half-a-dozen or more of the British India

---

[1] Warehouses.

Company's flotilla, and Patrick Henderson and Co.'s latest addition to their fleet. Other ships, steam tugs and lighters, and a multitude of sampans and small sailing craft add to the general effect of bustling commerce, the two principal items of which are impressed upon you by the large quantities of rice husks floating on the water, and the huge teak rafts of the Bombay-Burma Trading Corporation, Steel Brothers, and other merchants, drifting to their destinations at Elephant Point and elsewhere.

On landing, the first impression received is the *Indian* character of the place, for among all its varied nationalities the Indian native seems to predominate. The dock coolies, in simple loin-cloth and turban, are mostly Madrassees or Chittagonians, the " gharry "[1] and " tikka gharry "[2] wallahs half-bred Indians, while in the streets, ablaze with coloured costume, the dominant types are Hindus, Tamils, Madrassees, Cingalese, and Chinese. The Burman seems crowded out here, and has evidently been supplanted by his more energetic and active-minded rivals. Even the police in the streets are drawn from that fine body of men the Sikhs, while all the " chuprassies " or Government messengers are natives of India. The Chinese are largely in evidence. Most of the river carrying trade is in their hands ; quite the best shops and houses in the native quarters are theirs ; and their general good-humour and smile of quiet content testify to the prosperity they undoubtedly, and I think deservedly, enjoy. There is, of course, a large Burmese population in Rangoon, but they are

---

[1] Cart. [2] Hired vehicle.

Rangoon

mainly to be found in their own quarters, and on the bustling quay-side and business streets are less noticeable than their alien neighbours.

The men (other than Burmans) are on the whole good-looking, and, while the women of Ceylon and India are usually handsome, few of the Burmese women I saw in Rangoon can claim good looks, though quaint costume, beautifully dressed and glossy hair, and general vivacity of manner render them attractive.

Like its population, the town itself is cosmopolitan in style. Many of the more important buildings are fairly imposing, some even good, in architecture, but as a rule they are the square-built stucco houses common to the Levant, and I suppose the East generally, much the worse for wear (no doubt due to monsoon rains), and with the inevitable green "jalousies," usually rather "wobbly" and badly in need of a coat of paint.

In plan, Rangoon is well laid out. Main streets run parallel with the river front, intersected at right angles by others. These streets are wide and well metalled. Most of them are bordered by trees, an excellent provision in a country whose shade temperature even in the *cool* season runs up to ninety degrees.

In the centre of the town is Fytche Square, a pretty garden of considerable extent, around which are many banks, merchants' offices, and the principal shops, the whole being dominated by the beautiful cupola of the Sulay Pagoda.

Among the more important buildings in Rangoon is the new municipal market, an ornate structure of

Burma

considerable size, and to which the natives have taken kindly, though the bazaars still flourish, and to the artist at any rate offer greater attraction. Many odd nooks and corners of extreme interest are to be found: the Burman and Hindu temples of Pazundoung, the Chinese joss-house at the north end, the shops of the silversmiths and umbrella-makers, as well as the fruit bazaars in the front, while the Chinese and Japanese streets have each their special interest. All this is very fascinating, but is hardly *Burmese.* In fact, in the streets and bazaars of Rangoon the Burman might almost be regarded as the stranger, and only in the Shwe Dagon Pagoda and a few quarters peculiar to themselves do you find the Burman pure and simple, or at any rate have opportunity for studying him free from the overcrowding, noise, and activity of the other races.

The new-comer is almost immediately struck by the difference between the beasts driven by Burmans and those of other nationalities and religions. The Burmese cattle are *always* sleek, comfortable, and well fed; while those of the Mohammedan races are, as a rule, overworked and often cruelly abused. Here, perhaps, is a clue to the reason of the Burman being so completely overshadowed in his own place. Innately gentle, the same instinct and religious obligation which lead him to treat his animals with consideration hardly fit him to compete with the aggressive and noisy cupidity of others, whose one aim would seem to be to extract as much as possible from either man or beast.

Behind the commercial town lie cantonments, the

Rangoon

residential districts, the drive out being a very interesting one. All the roads are shaded by avenues of padouk, tamarind, banyan, and palms ; while the gardens, often bordered by hedges of feathery bamboo, are well stocked with tropical growths, among which are many handsome trees and shrubs imported from other countries. Through the hedges may be seen glimpses of flowers and pretty lawns, and the well-built timber bungalows are roomy and often handsome in design. Everywhere are evidences of wealth among the residents, and, by the way, of good government on the part of the municipality, the roads being wide, well kept, and watered, while the public gardens are tastefully laid out and maintained.

The hospitality of Rangoon is proverbial,—my own experience compels me to term it unbounded,—and a few days after my arrival I found myself surrounded by a circle of friends, a member of its leading clubs, and, with my servant, luxuriously installed in the bungalow of a high Government official in the Prome Road, and with all the advantages and opportunities for working which the solicitude of my host was able to afford me. I had been quite comfortable at the hotel, and have often fared worse in more pretentious establishments nearer home ; there is, however, this disadvantage in living in "town," that your environment is entirely the business element, which is so largely composed of alien races that "Burma" is eliminated from your view. Living in cantonments, however, with its purer air and more reposeful conditions, was very pleasant and the day's work relatively easy, while the Burman proved more easily discoverable than in the commercial centre, and at the same time under conditions which better suited his temperament. As the roads in the suburbs are well wooded and pleasant for promenading, here and in Cantonment Gardens, as well as the public parks, the Burmese lady, gay in coloured silks, is fond of walking with her no less daintily clad children. In the neighbourhood are many Burmese villages with their quaintly carved "kyaungs"[1] and "zeyats"[2]; but above all you are in close proximity to that wonderful building, the central and most sacred shrine of Buddhism, not only in Rangoon but throughout the country, the great Shwe Dagon Pagoda.

Here at last you find the Burman in his purity, and amid surroundings which are entirely complimentary, and much of my time in Rangoon was spent upon its platform, charmed but bewildered.

I find it increasingly difficult to give any adequate idea of this marvellous building, which Edwin Arnold fitly describes as a "pyramid of fire." It is simply wonderful, and impossible of description. As, however, this, the greatest of all Burmese pagodas, is but a glorified example of the rest, I must make the almost impossible attempt to describe it.

First let me say that there are two principal forms of temple in Burma—the "thein" or square-built temple, which is often surmounted by cupolas and

---

[1] Pronounced "choung"=a monastery.
[2] A rest-house for pilgrims and travellers.

pinnacles, as we will presently see among the ruins of Pagan ; and the "zedi" form, as here.

Viewed from a little distance, the Shwe Dagon is a graceful bell-shaped form rising above the trees which clothe the mound on which it is built, the apex being surmounted by a "ti" or umbrella, a graceful finial of wrought-iron overlaid with gold and studded with precious stones. From it depend little bells and cymbals which tinkle prettily as they swing in the breeze. The whole of this dome is gilt, a large portion being covered with plates of solid gold, and it may be imagined how glorious is the whole effect as it blazes under an Indian sun. A rather effective introduction of a single band of silver in one of its upper courses only adds to the richness of its appearance.

Four ascents, one from each cardinal point, lead to the platform from which the pagoda proper rises. Of these, that from the south is the most important. Formerly this entrance was perhaps the most striking architectural feature in the country. A broad flight of steps leads to a platform or terrace bounded by an ornamental wall ; passing between two enormous leogryphs, a further flight of steps and shorter terrace lead to a doorway of Gothic form, richly embellished by figures of "Nats"[1] and "Beloos"[2] in high relief, the arch being surmounted by a characteristic "pyathat." Beyond rise in succession the carved roofs of various bazaars which mark the different levels of the hill, the whole perspective culminating in the glowing mass of the Shwe Dagon itself.

[1] Gnomes.   [2] Devils.

Burma

Quite recently (it was only finished in 1903) this terrace has, at enormous cost, been covered in by a "tazaung,"[1] which, though handsome enough in itself, is in my opinion an unforgivable act of vandalism, as it entirely obliterates a view of an interesting and picturesque procession of historic structures which was quite unique.

The interior of this covered ascent is full of interest both architectural and human. On either side are stalls for the sale of anything, from candles and artificial flowers for presentation at the shrines to jewellery and toys. In fact it is probably the best bazaar for "odds and ends" in Rangoon ; and as the steps are steep, and crowded with gaily clothed passengers moving up and down through odd effects of light and shade, the whole forms, I think, one of the best pictures I saw in Burma.

Ascending the steps, you finally emerge from the half-light on to the sun-bathed platform (a huge circular space of many acres) which surrounds the base of the golden pile which towers 370 feet into the air.

Here again modern addition has somewhat marred the general effect of the building, the indiscriminate building of additional shrines upon this platform having almost hidden the plinth of the pagoda, so that the general sense of its proportion has been lost. Each of these shrines, however, is in itself so interesting, and so lavish in its decoration, that one is reconciled to their intrusion by a study of their own intrinsic merit.

Whether it be in their general design, elaborate carving, or glass mosaic, the number and size of the

[1] Pavilion.

ASCENT TO THE SHWE DAGON

Rangoon

Buddhas in bronze or alabaster they enclose, their enormous bells and ornamental " tis," every bit of these structures and their adjuncts is absolutely interesting and beyond my powers of description. The whole effect is one of golden splendour amidst which a throng, clad in all the most delicate tints of silk, move like scattered petals from a bouquet of roses.

Before the shrines are groups of devotees kneeling, or in the position of "shikoh," some with rosaries, others with flowers between their palms; they pray fervently, while lighted candles gleam before the niche from which a gilded Buddha smiles.

They appear very devout, and the hum of many voices joined in earnest supplication is impressive. Yet I am informed that the Buddhist prays " to nobody and for nothing " ! This may be so, and the Buddhist faith is one which few have been able to fathom ; but the sight of these evidently sincere worshippers would seem to contradict this negative assertion, and at any rate presents a striking instance of that dependence the human heart must always instinctively feel when contemplating the omniscient and the unknown.

These shrines are not for Burmans only, however. Buddhists of all races are represented, and all are dressed in gala costume. On festivals the Indian Buddhists particularly are richly clad : in one group which I noticed, the women, who were closely veiled, in addition to their other ornaments wore shields of silver on their toes. Each race or tribe appears to affect a particular shrine, which no doubt accounts for the erection of so large a number, but I was glad to learn that any further building on the pagoda platform has now been prohibited.

On the outer circle of this platform are many other buildings—offices for the custodian and his assistants, a library and Chinese temple, sundry shrines and "zeyats" for pilgrims, between which are stalls and booths for the sale of food-stuffs and votive offerings. Away in a corner, shaded by a pepul tree, are the graves of our officers who fell at the storming of the pagoda ; and not far away, in a half-ruined and neglected shrine, is the most beautiful figure of Buddha I have seen, in which the face, admirably modelled, really combines in its smile something of human sympathy together with the eternal peace of heaven. On the platform are two particularly good Shan "tis" beautifully wrought in perforated iron, also two others of stone, and a really fine "tagundaing," or flag-staff, the pediment of which is in five stages, each embellished with carved representations of dragons, garuda birds, ghouls, ogres, and fairies, in the order given. Among the many curios safeguarded by the custodian is a silver model of the Sulay Pagoda in which is enclosed a tooth of Gaudama, a relic supposed to be genuine, while facing the principal shrine two life-sized figures of teak, a man and a woman, in all the bravery of gaudy paint and tinsel, are dancing to the accompaniment of two gramophones which bellow forth in a noisy rivalry the latest comic songs from the London music halls ! It is all very incongruous but deeply interesting: everywhere is

Rangoon

some object to claim attention or admiration, to excite sympathy or amusement, but what at first puzzled me most was the great number of *bells* in every corner of the temple. Some of these bells are of enormous size, canopied by a handsome "pyathat"[1]; others of less size are in the open, suspended by handsomely wrought slings and bosses of bronze between their coloured posts. Beside each bell is a deer's antler with which to strike it, and I was informed that it is the custom for Buddhists, after praying, to strike first the earth and then the bell in order to draw the attention of the "Nats" of the nether and upper worlds to their act of piety! In all Burmese pagodas bells figure largely, and I think, without exception, each temple is also adorned by huge leogryphs as guardians of the entrance. The legend is that in the misty past a king's daughter was stolen by a forest "Nat" and hidden in the woody fastnesses. All attempts at recovery failed, until one day a lioness rescued the princess and restored her to her father. Since then the lion, conventionalised in course of time into the leogryph, has been perpetuated as the symbol of protection and guardianship.

Ever fond of a joke, the Burman likes to point out in the case of the Shwe Dagon Pagoda that one of these guardian effigies has a *sharp* tongue, while that of the other is *blunt*; one, they say, is a female, the other a male, but as to which is which the visitor is left to decide!

It is impossible in a short space to fully appreciate

[1] A canopy of five or seven roofs in diminishing scale terminating in an elongated finial.

all the interest of this most wonderful temple, which, in spite of certain incongruities, must impress even the most casual visitor with a feeling of admiration and respect for a religion which so beautifully expresses its devotion, and here alone in all Rangoon one gets a glimpse at the heart of Burma itself, and already begins to feel a sympathy with the people.

As a Burmese crowd may be as well studied at the Shwe Dagon as elsewhere, we might examine them a little more closely before leaving the pagoda.

All are gaily clothed. The men, who wear their hair long like a woman, are dressed in silk head-scarf or turban, a white jacket, and a kind of skirt, usually of coloured silk. These skirts are of two kinds : one a simple sack called "lungyi," twisted into a knot at the waist ; the other called "petsoe," a somewhat similar garment, but plus several yards of extra material which is either bunched up in front of the waist or serves as a head-and-neck shawl should it be cold. Most of the men in Rangoon wear boots, and carry cheap cotton parasols, which on the coast are supplanting the more picturesque native article.

In type the men are distinctly Mongolian and sallow in complexion, they wear a slight moustache and sometimes beard, and all (women included) smoke abnormally large cigars.

The women are infinitely more attractive than the men and less Mongoloid in appearance, the complexion being more ruddy, the cheek-bones not so high, and their features generally more regular. Their hair, which

Rangoon

is a purple black, is very luxuriant and always well
dressed. It is usually worn in a tight coil on the top
of the head, and in it is placed, in a very coquettish
manner, a rose or orchid or some other flower. In the
front of the coil is generally an ivory or white-wood
comb.

Their costume is much the same as the men's (except
that no head-dress is worn), the same dainty white
jacket and coloured "lungyi," or, in the case of those
of superior position, a "temaine," a skirt of greater
length so that it trails upon the ground, and which is
open at the side, exposing the leg nearly to the hips in
walking.

Round the neck, or thrown loosely over the shoulder,
is a scarf of figured silk usually bright in colour, and
on the feet sandals, or pattens, of wood.

Their gait is modest and whole appearance attractive,
and as they wander about, shaded by their quaint semi-
transparent umbrellas, chatting and laughing, flirting
their fans prettily, or enjoying their cigars, they form
the merriest and most fascinating crowd imaginable.
Yet they are devout, praying often at the shrines, and
are the business mainspring of the country. In fact,
the women seem to monopolise the brain and energy
of the race, and occupy an absolutely independent
position. The men are inclined to laziness, but *all*—
man, woman, or child—are good-humoured, happy, and
polite.

CHAPTER II

As I have already indicated, society in Rangoon is pleasantly environed, and the evidences of prosperity everywhere apparent are by no means at the expense of beauty.

The well-built bungalows are generally pleasing in design, and in many cases are made really pretty by flowering creepers and well-selected shrubbery. The "compounds" are large. Behind the bungalow, and screened from sight, are the stables and kitchens, the latter being connected with the house by a covered passage, a necessary provision against the monsoon rains. Before and about the house is the garden proper, generally well supplied with shade trees, while many are ablaze with bedded-out plants and flowering shrubs. Some of these gardens indeed are charming, combining all the wealth of the flowers and foliage of the tropics with the familiar and homelike annuals of the mother country ; geranium and pansy emulate the more pronounced glories of the cactus or bougainvillea, while violets modestly add their offering of perfume to that of the magnolia or lily.

Burma

The gardeners are always natives of India, and to give an illustration of the loving care with which they perform their duties, I may instance the lawn which was the chief glory of my host's domain, and in which each root of grass had been separately planted by his " mahli."

While glimpses of the gardens in these cantonments are often charming, some of the vistas afforded by its shady avenues are no less beautiful, with their mingled contrast of heavy foliage and delicately graceful branches and leaves. And the life of the roads themselves is always interesting and colourful : Indian coolies hurry along with their curious ambling gait, bearing baskets of cocoa-nuts or dishes of sweetmeats slung from the bamboo which they carry across their shoulders ; and Indian women, with their delicate little faces and small hands and feet (much be-bangled) appearing from out the folds of their red " saries." Chinese labourers, in huge straw hats and loose-fitting garments, go to their work smiling and ever ready to make a joke of any mishap which may befall them. Quaint gharries drawn by patient and mild-eyed bullocks convey daintily clad Burmese ladies to some social function or pleasure party, while at almost every corner are smart native police-men who salute the " sahib " as he passes.

The types are interesting, and give the scene the necessary touch of orientalism, and, as usual, the costumes are bright in colour. Pink appeared to be the favourite tint, but many combinations are worn, such as a scarlet coat with purple sleeves, pink skirt with apple-green shawl, etc., while, aided by the power-ful sunshine, colours which the Western mind would at once condemn as impossible of combination are here successfully and harmoniously blended.

In the previous chapter I have made use of the term "shikoh," which is the Burmese form of salute. In its full elaboration a squatting position is assumed with the hands placed palm to palm as though praying ; the hands are always pointed towards the person saluted, and should he move his position the Burman will alter his own so as to continue facing him. Indoors, shoes are always removed at the threshold as a first mark of respect. If met in the street, the Burman will lower his umbrella, place whatever he may be carrying on the ground, and "shikoh" in proper form. A modified and now more general form of "shikoh" is simply to place the hands together and bow to the person compli-mented. Another mark of respect is to approach the person to be saluted and touch his knee with the hand.

One of the unfortunate effects of our occupation of Burma has been the gradual undermining of this ancient courtesy, and in Rangoon the "shikoh" is almost a thing of the past ; and I was struck by the fact that, while all the other native races here are polite and respectfully "salaam" the European, the Burman alone declines to "shikoh" to any one, passing by with an air of unconscious indifference.

The young Burmans of to-day are beginning to wear socks and patent-leather shoes, and smoke American cigarettes. Inheriting the conceit of their forefathers, but without their inherent gentility, they decline to salute any one unless compelled to do so. In Rangoon this question recently became acute when the pupils in the schools, taking advantage of their mixed birth, struck against "shikohing" to their teachers, and the Government, somewhat weakly I think, gave way upon the point and substituted the military form of salute for the more picturesque native custom.

Apropos of this decline of native politeness you will sometimes hear a Burman object to do certain work on the score that he is a "trouser-wallah" (that is, that he wears European clothes) and is superior to any work. On the other hand, in country districts particularly, politeness on the part of the native is often carried to excess. Let me give an instance. A friend of mine was trying a new pony, which ran away with him, and in the narrow road overtook a cart in which were a family party out holiday-making. The pony ran into the back of the cart and threw his rider into the midst of the startled merry-makers, half-killing the Burman who was driving. Before my friend had time to offer any explanation of his unexpected onslaught, the Burman "shikohed" to him and said apologetically, "My lord, my lord, the cart should not have been there"!

While the Burman will often pay so much respect to the white man it is rather curious to notice that salutations between natives who may happen to meet in the road are rare, and even in the heart of the forest they will pass each other without so much as "Good day."

Every one in Rangoon is up with the sun, and after a very light "chota-hazri" is out walking or riding in the cool of the morning. By 9 A.M. a cool verandah with a lounge chair under a "punkah" is a refuge to be desired. The peculiar potency of the sun is remarkable. I do not think I noticed any temperature over 101° in Rangoon, while more generally 95° was about the maximum at mid-day, yet even in the relatively cool mornings a silk suit and solar topee were imperative. In Egyptian deserts I have been happy in a cloth cap and riding-suit with the thermometer far above these figures, but in the lower latitudes of India the angle of the sun's rays seems to impart to its *light*, as apart from its *heat*, a curious power of penetration from which protection is essential.

I was assured on arrival that it would be quite impossible for me to work out-of-doors during the heat of the day, even the animals taking their siesta, and for the first few days I sought sanctuary indoors between the hours of 11 and 4.

I was in despair as I saw how slowly work progressed, so taking my courage in both hands for the rest of my stay in Burma I worked consistently right through the day. Certainly this was very trying, and it required all one's determination to face the heat and glare, but I found it quite a possibility, and in and about Rangoon especially shade of some kind was usually obtainable.

I found the people most polite. If I happened to be

working near a building, a chair and umbrella would invariably be offered, and the Sikh policemen especially seemed to like to assume control of the crowd which, with mild and respectful curiosity, gathered round me to see what I was doing.

Sport of all kinds appeals to the European element in Rangoon; golf, tennis, cricket, or rowing on the lakes. Its parks are beautiful, and delightful excursions for riding or driving abound in its vicinity and serve to ease off the strenuosities of a hard day's work. Without entering upon any detailed account of the social life of Rangoon, charming though it be, I would like to describe shortly one common rendezvous much frequented in the evenings before dinner, and that is the Gymkhana Club.[1]

Hardly perhaps a club in the strict sense, it is a very general and popular meeting-place in the early evening. The building is large and airy, well supplied with card and reading rooms, the ground-floor being almost entirely occupied by its fifteen or sixteen billiard-tables. In front is the cricket-field, where many hard fights take place, but at this hour the lawn is given up to the children and their ayahs, and dotted with the tea-tables of members and their wives. Behind are tennis-courts and stabling. The ladies have their own reading and billiard rooms, and once a week an impromptu dance takes place in the recently added ballroom.

Altogether it is a breezy, jolly club, most generous in admitting strangers and displaying in a marked

---

[1] The Club has been entirely rebuilt and enlarged since my visit, but is not, I hear, quite so much frequented as formerly.

Amenities of Rangoon

degree that hospitality and good-fellowship which in my experience is so general a characteristic of the Anglo-Burman. It was here that, a few days after my arrival, I witnessed a novel proof of the tropical character of Rangoon. The monsoon rains had hardly yet ceased, and the air was filled with a steamy warmth which, in spite of punkahs and wide-open verandah-screens, rendered coats and waistcoats intolerable. The billiard-tables were all occupied, the markers being mainly employed in sweeping off the thousands of insects which, attracted by the lights, settled on the tables. These were of all kinds : curious hard and horny creatures, big grasshoppers, gaudy moths, twig insects, and the lovely leaf mantis—in fact, the collection of entomological specimens on the tables was far more interesting than the game. Finally the swarms of insects became so great that it was difficult to force a ball the length of the table, and the games had to be abandoned and all lights extinguished for a time.

Running all over the walls were lizards, pretty cream-coloured things which darted about catching moths and white ants, and chirruping to each other the while like sparrows, and in the dark corners lurked others, larger and greyer, of sinister aspect and suspicious movements, which rendered them open to the imputation of cannibalism. In a friend's house also I made the acquaintance of the well-known "tuk-too," a little lizard of some six inches in length, who calls his name explosively, and loudly enough to be startling on the first occasion. The "tuk-too" is considered lucky in a house and is never disturbed, and the natives regard it as poisonous, though this is not probable. Once in my bath-towel I discovered a large tarantula spider, and on another occasion disturbed a cobra in the grass, but with these exceptions I met with nothing dangerous to health or life in Rangoon, and even the mosquitoes were hardly noticeable.

Still there are snakes in plenty in the gardens, and it is always wise to have a lantern if walking after dark. I heard of a case, which I believe to be authentic, of a lady in Pegu, who, on leaving the local Club to walk to her house a very short distance away, trod upon a Russell's viper in the grass which fringed the road ; she was immediately struck in the ankle, and unfortunately died before she could reach her home. This, however, is an unusual case, and though general precautions are desirable I do not think the visitor to Rangoon need concern himself greatly about snakes.

Many pretty birds frequent cantonments : wrens and robins, doves and bulbuls, and the wearisome " coppersmith " bird, whose reiterated note, sounding like the stroke of a hammer upon copper, is often exasperating, especially in the heat of the day.

Like all Eastern towns Rangoon has its particular plague, and when I was there crows were the trouble. During the day they scavenge or thieve in the bazaars, but it is in the evening that the visitor is struck with amazement at their number and sagacity. Their rookeries are miles away in the jungle ; every morning they invade the town in their thousands, and at sunset return to their forest habitat. The sight as they fly home-wards is remarkable, and for an hour at least the sky is black with the continuous flight of these birds, which had lately increased in number so much as to become a serious nuisance in Rangoon, and their extermination, or at least limitation, a problem which was seriously exercising the minds of residents.

A chapter might be written about the Rangoon crow, but let me give one instance of his sagacity. A gentle-man residing in cantonments made a bet with a friend that he would, from his compound, shoot one crow nightly for a month. The first evening he bagged his bird, and on the second another, but on the third and every successive evening each flight of crows as it neared his residence soared until out of range, and, when the danger zone was passed, descended again to their normal level. How the warning was passed from one rank to another is a mystery, but it is the fact that our friend never got another shot.

It is inevitable that in a prosperous centre such as Rangoon much that is pictorial must give way to the necessities of modern improvement. Recently a Burmese village near the cemetery has been entirely swept away and its site added to the new Victoria Memorial Park, and nobody could deny how greatly the community benefits by the change. In many of the main thorough-fares are quaint nooks wherein Burmese life still lingers in its primitive simplicity, but which are just as inevitably doomed.

There is one village, however, which lies close to the

Burma

Shwe Dagon Pagoda on the road to Kokine which I trust will be permitted for many years to come to continue its picturesque and placid existence, and remain as an interesting link with a phase of life fast disappearing from Rangoon.

This is the village of Ngadatgyi-Hpya, more commonly known as Wingaba or the Labyrinth. People pass it daily in their drives, and though probably all admire the richly carved kyaungs which, half buried in a profusion of vegetation, fringe the road, few care to explore the winding lanes and causeways which lie behind and from which the village derives its name. It is a place of considerable sanctity, occupied mainly by hpungyis and pilgrims who have come from all over the Buddhist world to worship at the great shrine under whose shadow it is built.

I only visited it once, but then under conditions that have impressed the romantic aspect of the place vividly upon my mind. The occasion was the casting of one of the huge bells the Burmans love so much, a ceremony of religious importance and one for which great preparations are made. I elected to pay my visit the evening before the actual ceremony of casting, when the European element would be less in evidence, my host driving me over after dinner to the neglect of a dance to which we were both engaged.

Leaving our "tum-tum," or dog-cart, in the road, we turned into the lane to the village. It was bright moonlight, in which the paths gleamed white, while across them fell the black shadows of the palms and jungle

Amenities of Rangoon

trees which bordered them, and among which were zeyats and hpungyi-kyaungs, and many other booths and temporary buildings erected for the occasion. Emerging from mysterious depths of gloom and moving through these alternations of light and shade were animated groups of Burmans, whose costume, always picturesque, gained an additional and bewildering beauty of tone in the silvery moonlight,; and the ladies, having discarded the fans and parasols of day, wore, loosely thrown over their shoulders, shawls of both delicate tints and textures. As we ascended the sloping path towards the village the scene was one of extraordinary beauty, a tone study in which the opalescent tints which prevailed were further accentuated by the glare of an occasional lamp or the positive red of paper lanterns.

In the middle of the village is a sacred tank or lake, three sides of which are surrounded by forest trees and creepers ; on the fourth is the bazaar, which lined the road, with which it was level, though the rear of the buildings, supported upon piles, overhung the water of the lake. Every building was ablaze with coloured lanterns, and in the shops *anything* bright of tint was exposed for sale. Here and there were cafés, decorated with bright hangings, and filled with people whose beautiful dresses gained additional lustre from the many coloured lamps by which they were illuminated. Every one was in holiday mood—smoking, chatting, laughing, gay in colour, gay in temperament. It was delightful, and the general hilarity was further enhanced by the gambols of the youngsters, who, in paper

masks and grotesque costumes, played tricks upon the
passers-by. The road had now become a raised cause-
way of bricks, set herring-bone fashion, and presently,
by a flight of steps, mounted a hill deeply shaded by a
mango clump. Beyond was a series of hillocks and
dells upon which were built the monasteries and shrines
of the village itself. Facing us was a large white
building supported upon row upon row of columns
between which hundreds of devotees with lighted
candles "shikohed" before an enormous Buddha,
recently erected, and which could not have been less
than 40 feet in height. On first entering it was
difficult to see through the smoke in the dim light of
the candles (aided by a few electric lights), and it was
only after becoming accustomed to the semi-gloom that
one at last realised the presence of this enormous figure
which, calm, impassive, and with an air of benign
dignity, looked down upon you from the partial gloom
of the smoke-wreathed roof. When, however, the
consciousness of this extraordinary monument impressed
itself upon you the effect was instantaneous and impressive, and rendered the beholder oblivious to the
incongruity presented by the laughing holiday-makers
who, smoking and chatting, squatted in groups upon
the floor or moved indifferently among the worshippers.
Leaving this temple, we roamed about the causeways
which were built upon the ridges between the hills.
The hollows were occupied by booths in which all
kinds of "shows" were going on, each attended by a
crowd of jolly sight-seers. Many of these booths were

hung with curtains and formed the resting-place for the Burmese ladies who, squatting on the ground, were enjoying their cigars or the varied refreshments provided. In one was an exceedingly good marionette show accompanied by a Burmese orchestra, while two merry-go-rounds afforded amusement not only to the youngsters present but to many of their elders also. In the various kyaungs sat the village priests receiving the deferential salutations of the crowd and (incidentally) a varied assortment of presents. Some of these presents were curious, one I may mention being a handsome four-post brass bedstead, evidently just out from Birmingham, and which seemed to me to ill accord with the simple instincts and habits of the hpungyi. The whole scene was very animated : the contours of the undulations were plainly marked by the innumerable lanterns everywhere displayed, each hillock being crowned by a religious building or a clump of palm trees, while the little causeways which joined them swarmed with sight-seers.

On one of these knolls were the furnaces and mould for the enormous bell which was to be cast on the morrow. The arrangements were very simple. Four furnaces, built of bricks and mud, surrounded the mould itself, a very rough structure of the same material. The fires were all aglow, the blast being furnished by an enormous fan driven by a flywheel worked by hand, the air being led to the furnaces by pipes underground. By the side of each was a pile of copper, broken pots, etc., ready for melting, and I noticed that women in passing would frequently tear off their ornaments of gold and silver, sometimes set with stones, and throw them among the broken metal as their contribution to the smelting-pot.

The whole panorama, in which masses of gaily clad humanity, bewildering lights, and strange sounds were viewed under the romantic light of a tropical moon, formed a kaleidoscope as bewildering as it was fascinating, and I am afraid no words of mine can give an adequate impression of so strangely picturesque a scene.

It is rather sad to think that, after all this preliminary preparation, and the important public function which marked the day itself, through some fault in the mould the casting of the bell was a failure, and it had to be broken up. I have since been told that this particular bell weighed about 35 tons, and cost something like £1000.

The love of the Burmans for big bells is curious, the large bell in the Shwe Dagon Pagoda being about 40 tons in weight, while that of Mingûn weighs nearly 80 tons, with a diameter of 16 feet at the lip. None of them, however, are good in tone, and are not to be compared with the smaller bells or the exquisitely toned gongs for which Burma is so famous.

Though in no sense typical of Burma, Rangoon is in itself sufficiently interesting to warrant a much fuller description than I have attempted, but before leaving this subject let me say a few words about the Chinese, who are already a very considerable section of the

Amenities of Rangoon

Rangoon community, and destined, I think, to play an important part in the development of Burma. A large slice of the trade of the port is in their hands, and many of their merchants occupy positions in the municipal council and other posts of honour ; Mr. Tau San Kho, the Government archæologist, may be given as an instance, a cultured gentleman of charming and agreeable manner, to whom I am personally indebted for an interesting glimpse at Chinese life in Rangoon.

Their houses are quite the best and richest in the native town, and are gaily painted and decorated with hanging lanterns and beautiful vases containing flowers.

I noticed that invariably the woodwork was painted *red*, which, my guide informed me, was a "lucky" colour. Attached to the doors and window frames were strips of red paper inscribed in Chinese characters, all more or less tattered and weather-worn. These, it transpired, were the last year's New Year's Greetings of friends, the custom being to fix them to the doors, where they are left (again for "luck") until the next anniversary brings its fresh batch of good wishes with which to replace them.

Another point which attracts attention is the fact that the doors of Chinese dwellings are invariably in the centre of the house, they having a proverb to the effect that "luck comes in at the middle but runs out at the corners."

The Chinese have many curious superstitions, as a visit to one of their joss-houses will quickly demonstrate. Under Mr. Tau San Kho's escort I visited the new one at the north end, an exquisite little building which merits description. It is built on the river front, being set back from the street by an enclosed flagged square, which enables a good and uninterrupted view of the building to be obtained. The walls are of a kind of granite, greenish-grey in colour, and are broken by panels, in which are carved in low relief grotesque hunting scenes, or illustrations from the life of Confucius. Above are the curious up-tilted eaves and ridges of the series of roofs which cover the various chambers of the building. These roofs are of highly glazed tiles of many colours, greens, greys, and blues predominating ; the ridges terminate in finials composed of richly ornate dragons in porcelain, and between them are interspersed smaller figures of the same material. A flight of low steps leads to the entrance doors, which are guarded by finely wrought dragons in stone.

The interior is rich to a degree. Everywhere is ornamentation, the timbers are lacquered or carved like ivory, in some cases beams and joints being completely perforated almost like filigree work, and then picked out in gold and vermilion. The pillars supporting the roof are round, and composed of timber enamelled black, with inscriptions in gold running down them. At the end of the first court is a high altar, surmounted by a shrine containing figures carved out of wood, and in many parts of the building are ornamental vases containing flowers.

From the roof hang lanterns of wood, horn, or paper, each pretty or quaint, as the case might be.

Amenities of Rangoon

Nearly everything is painted red, and draperies of the same colour but of different tone, paper scrolls of an orange tint, and great splashes of brick red vary a scheme of colour, sumptuous yet harmonious, and to which the black columns and green and blue pottery act as a perfect foil.

This play of genuine vermilion is splendid, and, as though with studied effect, most of the worshippers wore black or grey costumes of a soft material.

I watched one man praying at the altar for a considerable time,—a curious sight. On the altar were vases containing a number of sticks carved and differently marked ; the " worshipper " shakes the vase in a peculiar manner until eventually *one* stick falls out and, according to its shape and markings, he interprets the answer to his prayer. There are also small pieces of wood, about the size of a small banana, round on one side and flat on the other, which are tossed into the air and fall clattering on to the floor ; if the flat side lies uppermost it signifies " good luck," if the round side " bad luck," and if one of each, just ordinary good fortune. The man I was watching was evidently meeting with indifferent success, for he continued to shake out sticks and toss for luck with the persistence, and, I must add, the *expression* of a gambler until in the end they fell as he desired, and he departed quite happy !

Round the central court is a corridor illuminated in cool tints, and opening out of this are a number of smaller rooms. One is a bedroom, another a restaurant, while in one was a stack of paper packets, each leaf being decorated and inscribed ; these, I learnt, were *prayers*, which are burnt in a stove in another room, together with the litter and sweepings of the temple! My cicerone presented me with a packet, the top sheet of which, I was told, is a prayer for " health, more money, and lots of children " ! My guide explained to me that " the English always like to have few children, one, two, or three perhaps, but we like to have lots and lots " !

The temple was pretty well thronged with people of all races and creeds, the Chinese being most tolerant of other religions, and " not like the Mohammedans and Hindus," as my friend observed. A further instance of this attitude was presented outside where, with their patterns marked on the pavement of the courtyard, a group of Indian fishermen were busy sail-making, " for, poor fellows, they could not do it in the street " !

This joss-house had only recently been completed, at the cost of £11,000, and every stick and stone of which it is composed was brought from China.

Though superstitious the Chinese are capable and industrious, easy to get on with, and ever ready to make light of their mishaps. They are good business men and hard bargainers, but once an agreement has been arrived at their given word is literally their bond, and may be implicitly trusted. Several times during my stay in Burma I was brought into close association with the Chinese, and soon found my inborn antipathy and misconception give place to a growing respect and real liking for a people often ignorantly maligned.

If, as unfortunately appears to be the case, the pure Burman is destined to disappear in favour of a hybrid race, I cannot help hoping that the preponderating alien blood will be Chinese rather than that of the more servile and less able native of India.

CHAPTER III

AMONG the many friends I made in Rangoon were the heads of the Bombay-Burma Trading Corporation, who kindly invited me to visit their forest of Taungdwingyi and see something of the teak industry and jungle life. Having purchased the necessary camp equipment I made a comfortable journey by the night train to Prome, accompanied by Mr. Maclennan, their forest manager. The first break of dawn found us running through paddy fields, pleasantly broken up by palm groves and clumps of forest trees, partly veiled by the morning mists which still hung heavy on the land. As we approached Prome station the first rays of sunlight were illuminating the golden pinnacles and dome of the Shwe Tsan Daw Pagoda, just visible through the palm trees which hid the base of the hill upon which it was built. It appeared very enticing, but as it was now 6.30 A.M., and we had to start by steamer at 7 A.M., Prome and its pagoda had to be reserved for a further visit.

As we entered the station Mr. Litchfield, of the

39

Burma

Survey of India, was waiting to receive us, and with the courtesy so typical of the country had prepared chota hazri for us, which his servants had brought to the station, and after a brief salutation and a hasty repast we started for our steamer.

On climbing the river-bank from the station, I do not think I ever saw a more beautiful view than this first glimpse of the Irrawaddy in the early dawn. The sun had only just risen, and the mists, floating in wreaths above the river, hung on the wooded heights on the other side or lay in the valleys like snowdrifts, the crests of the heavily wooded hills being lost to view. The river is wide, probably a mile or so, placid, deep, and swirling in eddies along the bank, now crowded with coolies transferring mails and baggage to the steamer.

The Irrawaddy is a noble stream, in the swift silence of its flow reminding me strongly of the Nile, though I missed the beautiful lateen-sailed boats of Egypt. There were few vessels on the river, though the dug-out canoes and an occasional " laung-zat "[1] moving slowly over its placid surface gave it a particular interest of its own. The eastern bank is not high, but on the western side the land rises in tiers of serrated hills to a height of probably three or four thousand feet. Every hill is heavily covered with growth, and the banks are beautiful with varied foliage, in which the feathery bamboo contrasts pleasingly with the denser habit of the forest trees, while the toddy palm rears its high

[1] A cargo boat.

crest in rivalry with the ever-present pagoda. Our steamer started promptly, the character of the banks varying little as we proceeded upstream, though the almost instantaneous disappearance of the morning fogs opened up more extended vistas, and enabled one to judge better as to the general characteristics of the scenery.[1]

On the river banks are Burmese villages constructed mainly of bamboo, while nearly every knoll is crowned by a pagoda or a monastery. On the sand-banks of the river are fishing huts, which will be washed away next rise, and at frequent intervals rafts of enormous size drift slowly towards the teak mills in Rangoon. Smaller craft of various kinds, under sail or drifting with the stream, together with the animated crowds which, in search of profit or amusement, thronged the landing-places at which we stopped, kept one's interest alive until, about sun-down, we reached the town of Thayetmyo. Here we had to transfer from the mail-steamer to a small ferry-boat, on which we spent the night.

Leaving early in the morning, a short run brought us to Meegyoungyai, where it had been arranged for coolies, bullock gharries, and ponies to be waiting to

---

[1] These jungle-clad hills are, I am told, full of game, and I heard of one particularly sportsmanlike event which took place hereabout. A gentleman coming down the river in a steamer, in searching the banks with his field-glasses, picked up what he took to be the trail of a rhinoceros, and persuading the captain to put him ashore, he with his "shikarri" followed the trail for several hours, eventually coming up with and killing a fine "rhino," the head of which he was able to take away.

transport us to the forest; and, our stores and kits having been landed, we found ourselves at about 4 P.M. comfortably installed in the dâk bungalow for the night. I noticed, by the way, that all the coolie work in connection with the landing of the cargo from the steamer was performed by women and girls (the men preferring to look on and smoke), and it was surprising what enormous weights even young girls were able to carry on their heads.

This village and dâk being typical, I may as well describe them here.

The village is built on the banks of the river, prettily situated among the groves of trees which overhang the pools below. On its other three sides is a high stockade of thorns, overgrown with yellow convolvulus and other creepers. At each side are gates, which are shut at night and placed under the charge of a guard, no one being allowed to pass after dark. Within the huge compound so formed are groves of toddy palms, mango, and tamarind, amongst which are the houses of the Burmans. These are usually built of bamboo, though many have their principal timbers of eng wood, all being raised from the ground on piles four to six feet in height as a safeguard against floods, snakes, and malaria. The floors are usually of split bamboo, the thatch of elephant grass, or "thekke"; bamboo mats, called "tayan," prettily plaited and often in coloured patterns, serve as walls, but as the side nearest the street is usually open the whole interior arrangements and domestic occupations are exposed to view. About the

Across the Yomas to Taungdwingyi

houses are the occupants, brightly picturesque, while the little boys and girls run naked. Pigeons and poultry, geese and dogs are everywhere, inside and underneath the houses, and the hot air is full of sweet nastiness from the Burmese kitchens. Generally speaking, the houses are more or less in line, forming streets, which are now busy with returning bullock gharries and driven cattle coming home for the night, as it is not safe for cattle to be left outside after sunset.[1]

The dâk bungalow lies outside the town, among a number of ruined pagodas, and stands in a stockade of its own. It is built much in the same manner as the Burmese huts, but is mainly composed of wood and stands higher. A flight of steps leads to the verandah, which is about 10 feet above the ground. This verandah forms the general living room, out of which are two bedrooms, each with a bath-room attached. The kitchen, stables, and servants' quarters are built in the compound outside. These dâks are built by the Government for the use of travellers, and have usually a Durwan or Kansammah in charge, and are supplied with such utensils as are absolutely necessary for comfort.

---

[1] All villages in Burma are stockaded, usually by a thorn zariba, or, in the case of hill villages, by chevaux-de-frise.

On each side is a gate made of heavy planks of teak, which run on wheels, and are by law closed at nightfall as a protection against both wild animals and dacoits. The villagers are compelled to keep guard at night, when no stranger is allowed to enter the village. Keeping guard is called "kin," the guard himself "kinthamah," and by the gate is usually erected a little booth, which serves as his sentry-box and is called "kinteaine." These stockades, overgrown as they usually are by many kinds of flowering creepers, have a very pretty effect.

Burma

The view from the bungalow looking across the Irrawaddy valley towards the distant Arracan Yomas[1] was exceedingly beautiful, green to the farthest distance with its first spring foliage.

The name Meegyoungyai, I was informed, means Alligator water, a title sufficiently appropriate, though I was later given another explanation, which I believe to be more correct, and which is certainly quaint enough to repeat. Long ago, says the legend, a huge alligator carried away a cow belonging to a poor farmer, who, in great distress, appealed to the forest " Nats " for assistance, which was readily forthcoming. One of these, assuming the form of a monkey, went down to the river bank and began to disport himself in the trees which overhung the pool in which the alligator was lying. Attracted by his antics and chattering, the alligator slowly came out of the water on to the bank, the better to watch him, but said nothing. Pretending to have just discovered the alligator's presence the monkey poured forth a torrent of derision and abuse upon him, but still the alligator remained silent. After a time the monkey suddenly exclaimed : " Why, it is not an alligator at all, it cannot even laugh." " Yes, I can," exclaimed the now exasperated saurian, and opening his wide jaws for that purpose out jumped the cow, which ran away up the bank into the forest, and was restored by the Nat to its owner. From that day the place has been called " Meegyoungyai " or " Laughing alligator," the word Meegyoung mean-

1 " Yoma " means literally " backbone."

THE IRRAWADDY VALLEY AT MEEGYOUNGYAI

ing alligator, and the terminal syllable, ye or yai, meaning "water or laughter," a very slight difference of intonation being the only possible difference between the two interpretations.

At one time Meegyoungyai must have been a town of some importance, a large number of pagodas still remaining, while far beyond the limits of the present village may be found traces of larger theins, shrines, and monastic buildings, so ruinous as to be hardly distinguishable among the undergrowth. One of these "kyaungs" is still occupied, and I was greatly struck by a pretty ceremony which takes place daily.

The sun had just set, and while preparing for our evening meal, the sound of a deep-toned gong stole through the warm air ; before its reverberations had ceased first one and then another was sounded, until perhaps twenty or more gongs of different pitches, but all with that purity of tone distinctive of the Burmese bronzes, combined in one swelling and melodious evensong. I inquired as to its meaning, and was informed that this was the usual "pyashikoh," the habits of the monastery being as follows. At first break of dawn all the priests, novices, and pupils assemble for prayer, after which the boys are occupied with their lessons. Meals are taken at 7 and 11.30 A.M., the priests being forbidden to touch food from 12 noon until after morning prayers the next day, the pupils, however, having their meals as usual. The day's work being finished, priests and pupils assemble in their different kyaungs, and to the sound of the first gong the lessons learned during the day are repeated. A second gong is the signal for general prayer; the third, in which all the gongs in the different monasteries are struck together, is the final Amen, and after this silence.

The day's work begins early in Burma : our usual custom was to take our chota hazri by candle-light at 4.30 or 5 A.M., so as to be ready for a start at the first flush of dawn, and, as all animals rest between ten and four o'clock, our journeys had to be made in the early morning or in the cool of the evening.

Leaving Meegyoungyai in the grey dawn our road lay over the Yomas, a gradually ascending tract of land covered with scrub jungle, and, excepting for occasional patches of Indian corn and sessamine, entirely uncultivated. There were few trees, and as the sun rose higher the dust and heat became very trying, no shade of any kind being obtainable. The grass was sunburnt and brown, and on the higher levels the few trees there were, were already in their autumn foliage. The scrub, however, was still green, and though the scenery generally could hardly be called beautiful, it had an interest to me in its strange flowers, new growths, birds and butterflies, which robbed the dusty journey of some of its tedium. Through the jungle enormous herds of cattle are roaming, all draught animals turned loose by their owners until required for transport purposes. All the cattle in the fields wear bells ; sometimes these are of bronze, but more generally of hard wood made in the form of an oblong box, in which hang four or more clappers. These serve the double purpose of locating the cattle as well as frightening away snakes as they browse. It was a lonely country, almost devoid of inhabitants, and one which dacoits were known to frequent. Indeed, the day before I rode over it a Government convoy had been attacked and robbed of several thousand pounds by a band in the vicinity. During our ride we met a second convoy consisting of two or three bullock-carts guarded by an escort of Sikhs. On approaching us bayonets were fixed, and with a great show of alertness the proper military salute was given. Otherwise we met little on the road except an occasional bullock train driven by Burmans, who in each case were polite enough to draw up their carts until we had passed lest we should be smothered in the dust. Altogether it is a hot and tedious journey, and I was very glad at the end of thirteen miles to reach the dâk bungalow of Thityahgouk, pleasantly situated among green fields 900 feet above the sea level.

Though the ride from Meegyoungyai remains in my mind as the least interesting I made in Burma, certain interesting facts recall themselves as I write. It was curious, for instance, to find in a district so sparsely inhabited and practically devoid of cultivation, a large number of pagodas, many semi-ruined and covered with creepers, and occasionally a yellow-robed priest praying at the shrine.

Here also I made acquaintance with the cutch tree, rather to my cost. My pony was flagging under the hot sun, and thinking a switch might aid matters, I rode up to a tree densely clothed with feathery foliage in order to break off a branch for the purpose. The hidden branches proved to be covered with a multitude of fine thorns, and I was obliged to let my pony wander on at his own pace while I devoted my attention to my lacerated fingers.

Among other trees I noticed was the teak, and one which I took to be blue gum, and cactus and aloes were plentiful. There were a fair number of birds, including doves, hoopoes, miners, wagtails, woodpeckers, green pigeons, and blue jays, and at Thityahgouk I saw a new species in the shape of a white vulture, occupied in tearing the dead leaves from off a toddy palm for nesting purposes.

In contrast to the dusty road we had just traversed, the view from the bungalow at Thityahgouk was like a glimpse of the promised land. From its high position on the crest of the Yomas the scene was an extended one. At our feet was the little village, so completely surrounded by its vine-covered barricade that only the highest roofs were visible from the outside. Beyond was a sea of foliage, forest trees covering ridge after ridge like green billows, over which the eye roamed from point to point delightedly.

In the distance, over this succession of verdure-clad hills, was the valley of the Sittang, plainly marked by the filmy haze which hung above the river. Beyond, the land rose in a further succession of hills, gradually becoming bluer as the distance grew, until on the

Across the Yomas to Taungdwingyi

farthest horizon, and across the watershed of the Salween could be plainly seen the crest of a noble mountain, which I was told was situated in Siam, 120 miles away. It was a splendid panorama seen under the best conditions, the air having been cleared by heavy showers which had fallen during the day, while the shadows of the monsoon clouds which hung above the land gave relief to its undulations.

We spent the night here in the dâk bungalow, where I was fortunate in meeting Mr. Long, a forest officer, who in our short evening together gave me a great deal of valuable instruction upon forestry, a subject upon which I have found great difficulty in obtaining accurate information. Unfortunately he was bound for Magwe, a day's ride in the opposite direction to my own, and I had not again had the pleasure or benefit of his companionship.

A rather tiring ride of twenty miles brought me to Taungdwingyi, the road being well metalled and rather harder going than the looser tracks of the jungle, but throughout well fringed with fine trees, and very much like a good country road in Somerset or Cheshire. At frequent intervals along the roadside were little thatched receptacles on poles called "yaiohzin," in which were jars of drinking water, the water-pots being kept constantly replenished by those living in the vicinity as an "act of merit." The drinking-cup is usually formed of polished cocoa-nut shell, with a long handle of some hard wood.

I noticed also that the distances were marked by

Burma

wooden posts every quarter of a mile, and this appeared to be the general rule on *made* roads throughout the country. By walking one mile and cantering the next we made good time, and in the early afternoon arrived at the comfortable and roomy bungalow of the Bombay-Burma Trading Corporation, on the outskirts of Taungdwingyi.

During these two days I made my first personal acquaintance with the Burman, for, with the exception of my own Indian servant, all our attendants were natives of the country.

I was much struck with the innate politeness which characterised them, their services being rendered quite naturally, and more with the air of an equal wishing to honour his guest than with the obsequiousness of the hireling, though at the same time with complete respect. Their voices, too, are pleasant, and their movements in the house and in attending to our wants at table had much of the natural grace of women. Indeed, so much is this the case at times, that, were it not for the head scarf which they wear, an adornment which the women do not affect, it would sometimes be difficult in the case of young men to determine their sex. I have been told, though with what truth I cannot say, that the universal custom of the male Burman to be tattooed from the waist to just above the knee was ordered by a former king in order to facilitate the instant recognition of the sexes. Whatever its origin, however, the custom exists, and many of the patterns with which their limbs are adorned are of the most ornate description.

Across the Yomas to Taungdwingyi

This ride also served to introduce me to the Burmese pony, which I found to be a hardy and sure-footed little beast, much like the Iceland pony in character, but like him badly bred. That fine ponies may be bred in Burma the large number of smart polo ponies to be found in Mandalay and elsewhere is ample proof, but, speaking generally, the ponies met with in the country are utterly lacking in points of breeding, and are often undersized.

The Burmese appear to be fond of their animals and, so far as I have seen, treat them well. One curious and cruel custom came under my notice here, however. After a journey the native administers a strong counter-irritant to fatigue in the shape of eye medicine, some irritating preparation being applied to the eyes of elephants, bullocks, and ponies after a hard day's work. These preparations are of various kinds, such as Chili pepper, ginger, or salt, powdered, and wet with spirits ; cloves and pepper, sometimes nutmeg, and asafœtida are also used, in fact almost anything calculated to make the animal's eye smart.

With regard to their ponies, the Burmans' pride seems to be in their tails, the length of which regulates the price asked. An instance occurred in Taungdwingyi which exemplifies this. During a " deal " between a Burman and an Englishman the price demanded was palpably excessive, the Burman laying great stress upon the length of its hirsute adornment. In a momentary spirit of mischief the Englishman quickly docked the pony's tail, exclaiming, "Now, will you take my offer?" "Take it away," cried the native in despair; "it is no use to any one now"; and he was then quite willing to accept almost any price offered, though the figure was eventually fixed at a fair and reasonable sum.

FIRST STEPS

CHAPTER IV

IN A BURMESE MARKET TOWN

STILL a village of considerable size, Taungdwingyi must at one time have been an important place, judging by the remains of its ancient walls and fortifications, and the large number of religious buildings, now mostly in a ruinous condition. The village is picturesque, and its approaches particularly are pretty. The roads are bounded by deep ditches, full during the monsoon, though now almost dry ; these are spanned by quaint wooden bridges, which lead to the dwellings of the natives. The streets are wide and grass grown, and form delightful pony tracks, of which the Burman is not slow to avail himself, and many trotting matches take place in these quiet thoroughfares. Trees abound in and about the village, avenues of banyan and tamarind alternating with groves of toddy palms.

The people are simply though nicely dressed, and the scenes on the road as they come and go are most characteristic. I never failed to experience a feeling of pleasurable surprise on seeing a daintily clad girl emerge from some humble thatched hut, looking so bright and clean, and arranging her silken scarf round her neck, or giving the final pat to her well-dressed hair before starting upon her promenade or errand. These people have so much that is innately pretty in their composition that nature itself seems to be beautified by their presence, and even the poorest have a peculiar faculty for arranging and wearing their simple garments to advantage.

I spent a week or more in this delightful village, the first I had actually lived in, and look back upon my time with sincerest pleasure. Its resident magistrate, Mr. Hill, did everything possible to assist my work and make my visit pleasant, while my friends of the Bombay-Burma Trading Corporation, Messrs. Maclennan, Smythe, and Skeene, were indefatigable in their efforts to ensure my comfort.

The homes of the people were much as I have already described, but I had more leisure here in which to notice their daily habits and occupations.

In the streets are the children playing with the " pi " dogs or making mud pies in the puddles. Little toy carts and peg-tops amuse some, while the boys are very fond of kite-flying ; but not content with simply winding the line round a stick, as our urchins do, they use a large drum revolving on a handle, rather like a magnified fishing reel. Toy boats and marbles are other amusements affected in the intervals of school, where squatting in rows upon the floor the lesson is recited in a sing-song manner, much after the fashion of our own board schools.

Through the open front of the houses the passer-

In a Burmese Market Town

by has many a pleasant glimpse of domesticity. In one, slung on cords from the roof beams, hangs a wicker cradle (called a " paket "), in which a pretty young mother gently rocks her child to sleep. Before another, or in some grassy lane, a would-be toddler receives its first lesson in walking ; all the young infants I noticed were carried astride the shoulder, as in Egypt. Young women come and go bearing pots of water or bundles of firewood, while their elders sit at their thresholds stitching up cotton " lungyis," or the more ornate silk " petsoe."

Attached to the houses is often a " lean-to " shed, in which cooking operations are carried on, and as usual in the space between the ground and the floor the live stock of the establishment finds its habitation.

Here also is one of the best - ordered and most interesting jails I have ever inspected, in which Mr. Hill took a very pardonable pride. Everything about the place was beautifully kept, and clean to a degree, while even the inner courtyards were planted with crotons and vegetables, only the well-kept gravel walks being used for prisoners' exercise. The jail, by the way, was more than self-supporting from the sale of its garden produce and the matting, baskets, and utensils manufactured by the prisoners.

As usual, the police were Indian military police, and it happened that their annual musketry training was going on while I was there. The range was just outside the town, the butts being part of an old " bund," and the target composed of a paper screen.

Burma

I found that the men were using smooth-bore Sniders with round bullets, the charge consisting of $2\frac{1}{2}$ drams of black powder. Of course such weapons had no great range, and were very erratic on account of "windage," but it was surprising what good practice the men made at 200 and 300 yards, scoring an average of "inners."

We Europeans took advantage of the targets being in position to organise a rifle meeting of our own, and though we used the service rifle and ammunition, I am afraid we hardly made so good a record as the policemen with their more primitive arms. It was a very pleasant episode, however, and I was struck with the good-fellowship existing among the men, and their evident affection for both the magistrate and their commanding officer, Mr. O'Donnell.

Close to the range is a secluded hpungyi settlement, among whose pretty kyaungs are fish ponds overhung with willows and rich in iris and lily, and, hidden away among the trees, is an ancient " thein " of strikingly good design and decoration, built of terra-cotta brick, but now entirely ruinous. I tried to ascertain something of its history and date, but no one was able to give me any information on these points. Behind the town is a large "jeel," or lake, covered with lotus and surrounded by reedy marsh-land, in which snipe and wild duck abound, and I gathered that game of many kinds is to be found in the immediate neighbourhood of the town, including sine, bison, barking-deer, and pig.

In a Burmese Market Town

Taungdwingyi, however, has an evil reputation for snakes, and the police records show an annual mortality from snake-bite of over 400. Though I had heard so much of reptile life in Burma I had, so far, not seen a single snake, and, in spite of a fairly careful search among its broken masonry and undergrowth, I failed to find any here. No doubt the noise caused by the heavy boots worn by the Europeans alarms them, while the barefooted native, coming upon them unawares, is too often struck.

A bazaar is held in Taungdwingyi every fifth day, people coming in from a wide area, together with numbers of professional peddlers who wander through the country. Every bazaar, therefore, in addition to the local population, is frequented by types from different parts of Burma.

The market-place is a large open space, enclosed by high wooden palings, within which are several permanent buildings as well as temporary booths composed of matting and coloured cloths. These are so arranged as to divide the market into sections, each more or less frequented by vendors of the different classes of goods and produce offered for sale.

All Eastern markets are more or less the same in general character, but this one struck me as being a particularly bright and animated scene, in which the fruit and vegetables exposed for sale were hardly less vivid in colouring than the costumes of the vendors, and a distinct local touch was given by the sunshades of paper or oiled calico carried by the women, or which, stuck into the ground, formed a grateful shelter for the stallholders.

Among the articles exposed for sale were saffron, betel nut, bananas, wild pineapples and papaya, as well as many other fruits and vegetables, among which, by the way, was the pumpkin-like fruit of the bael tree, the juice of which is supposed to be very efficacious in cases of dysentery.

The shops of the permanent buildings contained a curious assortment of wares : Burmese silks, Manchester cotton goods, Sheffield hardware, and school books and pencils from Germany ; curious wooden combs and pattens, and, what was always a source of special attraction to the ladies, cheap looking-glasses capable of a maximum of distortion.

Unwholesome-looking sweetmeats and cakes made of flour, " toddy," sugar, and spices, excite the wistful glances of the youngsters, and in all corners of the bazaar were stalls for the sale of food. In one, sausages and rice cakes simmer over a little charcoal fire, while from the next is wafted the delicious smell of sandalwood as a corrective. Roast meat, cut into small strips, is spitted on bamboo skewers, which are stuck all round the rim of a basket containing what at first sight appeared to be candles of unusual size. These, however, prove to be " sticks " of rice prepared in a curious way. A special kind of rice called " kowknyin " is placed in a green bamboo, together with a little water, the bamboo then being closed with a plug and put into the fire ; by the time the bamboo is dried and commences to burn the rice is cooked. The bamboo is then split, and the rice, beautifully cooked, is extracted in the compact form aforesaid.

Another curious dish I noticed was composed of flowers and red ants. The flowers are plucked when covered with ants, which feed upon them ; they are then put into salt and water and used as a flavouring for curry and other dishes. This also is supposed to have medicinal properties, particularly in the case of rheumatism and at child-birth. This dish is very sour in flavour, and is called " thargin."

One corner of the market was given up to the sale of earthen cooking pots, their bright terra-cotta contrasting well with the costumes and the greenish-grey baskets of bamboo which lie in all directions. Some of these baskets are of enormous size, and the designs of all are quaint and at times elegant. Another portion is occupied by the country carts, covered with their hoods of " tayan," and beneath whose shade the idlers of the market sleep.

Hpungyis, bearing a receptacle of burnished brass or vermilion lacquer, wander through the serried ranks collecting " sun " to the sound of a gong, while Karens and Shans, Chins and Kachins, as well as natives of India, give additional variety to a motley throng, which, however, is mostly purely Burman.

Although I had an interpreter with me, my ignorance of the language unfortunately prevented my full enjoyment of much of the humour of the bazaar. I was attracted, however, by the singular appearance of a middle-aged man, who, squatting on the ground, was dispensing medicaments. His hair was coiled very much on the side of the head, around which was wound his coloured "goungboung,"[1] one end of which hung over his ear in a jaunty manner, which belied his apparent age. He proved to be the village doctor, and the strange wares spread upon the cloth before him were no less curious than his own appearance. These consisted of boars' tusks and bits of bone, dried herbs, coloured stones, and the bark of various trees, little bottles containing powders and strange compounds, and various charms which, if I were to describe them, would, I fear, shock the susceptibilities of many of my readers, but from which I judged that his were largely *faith* cures based upon superstition. Here, in contrast, comes a lady arrayed in silks and attended by her companion, daintily testing the qualities of the fabrics she wishes to buy ; yet she is not above a vigorous use of the vulgate in the negotiations necessary to the occasion. In another place I saw a withered old lady dispensing a stew from a large pot by her side ; while conversing with her neighbours, a pony browsing through the market-place thrust his dusty nose under her arm into the pot, and managed to swallow a fair quantity of the contents. Hitting him on the muzzle with her ladle, the old lady indignantly waved the pony away, exclaiming, " Get away, pony, what do you think you are playing at ? " and then calmly proceeded with the sale of her concoction, which was apparently con-

[1] Turban.

A STREET IN TAUNGDWINGYI

sidered none the worse for the pony's intrusion. All over the place crows and hawks vie with "pi" dogs and half-naked urchins in scrambling for odd tit-bits, and almost above the hum of voices sounds the buzzing of flies as they struggle in the sticky sweetmeats.

After the glare of the open market it was pleasant to enter the central building, in which silks and the finer fabrics are mostly sold. It was very cool and shady, and at the junction of its four arcades is a large fountain, where the sound of the splashing water serves to increase a sense of coolness and refreshment.

Taungdwingyi is a great centre of the manufacture and the sale of silk, and at nearly every stall silks of different colours figure largely. These stalls are usually kept by women of good social standing, who, almost without exception, were good-looking and graceful. They did not appear to me, however, to be very intent on selling their goods, many of them being more occupied with their toilet, aided by one of the small mirrors aforesaid. The local silk, by the way, is of exceptionally fine quality, and I made several purchases here, which I have altogether failed to match in London. One might go on indefinitely describing the incidents of a village bazaar, and indeed it would be difficult to convey any adequate impression of a scene in which were combined brilliant colour, interesting faces, strange occupations, bustle and movement in bewildering confusion.

Altogether I found this bazaar most attractive, and I made many sketches here ; one corner only I found was to be avoided, and that was the portion of the market allocated to the butchers, who were nearly always natives of India, the Burmese being forbidden by their religion to take life in any form. A butcher's shop is never a very attractive sight, but here, in the hot air, alive with flies, meat surely never looked less attractive, while underneath and about the stalls "pi" dogs snarled and quarrelled for the garbage. The Burmans, however, are not squeamish, and were eager customers. Indeed, such is their greed for flesh that they consume every portion of the carcase, the intestines included.[1]

My time in Taungdwingyi passed all too quickly; I found it an exceedingly agreeable place in which to work, while the companionship afforded by the few Europeans resident in the village was very pleasant. On most afternoons I was accompanied by one of my friends, and it became a habit with us when work was finished for the day to drop into Mr. Hill's house, where, whether he was at home or not, "pegs" would always be brought to us by his bearer, while we lounged on long chairs on the verandah and amused ourselves with his gramophone. I never before realised the power of amusement embodied in this somewhat despised instrument, yet, as we were far away from other forms of entertainment, a banjo quartette or a song from an

---

[1] Later on, in the forest, I heard also of cases where elephants which had died of anthrax and been buried, had been afterwards exhumed and feasted upon by Burmans !—disgusting orgies, to put a stop to which the Bombay-Burma Trading Corporation now in all cases cremate the bodies of any animals which may happen to die, from any cause whatever.

opera, even as rendered by a gramophone, was a real source of enjoyment.

In Taungdwingyi also I experienced one of those delightful *rencontres* which are among the many attractions of travel. I had, just as usual, come in from my day's work when a new arrival appeared in the shape of a mud-bespattered and very hot " shikarri," just come in from a day's snipe-shooting. I was rather surprised to hear the exclamation : " Hullo, Kelly, who expected to see you here ! " I then discovered him to be Captain Moffat, of the King's Own Scottish Borderers, then stationed at Thayetmyo, whose friendship I had made many years ago when his regiment was quartered in Egypt. We had a long chat over old friends and places, followed by an invitation to visit his mess when next I was on the river,—an invitation I warmly accepted, and of which I was fortunately able to avail myself shortly afterwards.

While waiting for the preparations for our forest journey to be completed, my friends had arranged a " pwe " for me, which was given on the last evening I spent at Taungdwingyi.

These " pwes " are the national plays of Burma, and are of three kinds :—

1. The zappwe, or drama, in which men and women perform.

2. The hanpwe, or ballets.

3. The yotthepwe, or marionettes.

Of these, the second is entirely performed by young girls, amateurs, who, dressed in court costumes, perform the conventional dance of Burma to the accompaniment of an orchestra, which I will presently describe. Their drill is perfect, and their sense of time and rhythm as they move together quite extraordinary. This performance always takes place during the day, and is considered one of the most beautiful pageants in Burma.

The performance arranged on my behalf, however, was the zappwe, or drama, performed by professional actors engaged by my hosts.

In the compound in front of the bungalow a rough stage of bamboo draped with coloured cloths had been erected, and towards sun-down people began to arrive for the performance, every one being welcome on these occasions. Practically all the village came, some walking, some driving, and took up their positions in a large semicircle facing the stage, in the centre of which chairs had been placed for us.

By 7.30 (dinner-time) the performers arrived, and commenced to dress for their parts in front of the large audience which had gathered, the tedium of waiting being further relieved by the tuning of the instruments of the orchestra.

As these " pwes " continue for an interminable length of time, the outside of this ring of spectators gradually assumed the appearance of a bazaar. Fires were lit and stalls erected for the sale of hot coffee, cakes, curry and rice, and a variety of stews. Outside these was a ring of bullock-gharries occupied by women of superior position, with their children, many of whom

were quite naked, others being simply wrapped up in a lungyi.

Next to the stage were the musicians, eight in number, now busy tuning up. The instruments used are peculiar and deserve description. First is the "sine," a circular "tub" with perforated and carved sides, round the inside of which are suspended on strings two octaves of drums, or tom-toms, covered with black goat skin. These are tuned by clay being squeezed on to the skin until the right pitch is reached. The skilful manner in which the operator manages the clay is interesting to watch, and it forms a pretty pattern in white upon the dark skin. These drums are called "patlongyi," and are played with the flat of the fingers, the musician sitting in the middle of the ring. The "chenoungwine" is a similar instrument, which stands higher and in which circular bronze gongs take the place of the drums. Each of these gongs, or "chenoung," is tuned by pouring from behind a little melted wax into a boss or projection in the centre. Once tuned they retain their pitch, and the other instruments are periodically attuned to them. Here also the player sits in the middle of the gongs, which entirely encircle him, and uses a small drumstick, with which, by a quick backward turn of the wrist, he strikes those behind him with equal facility to the others. There is also a big drum called "patmagyi," and the smaller "boundouk," both of which are struck with the open palm ; large cymbals called "legwin," and a smaller pair called "thanlwin." The "waletkok" is a clapper made of bamboo, and the full band of eight is completed by the "hne," a reed instrument rather like a flageolet, but with a large bell mouth of brass. The tone of this "trumpet" is rather strident, but, modified by the softer and more melodious "sine" and "chenoungwine," the orchestra combined in producing music, which, if somewhat barbaric, was pleasing in its general effect, and I think quite the best Eastern music I had heard.

After half an hour's overture the play began, but as it was performed in court language, which few but Burmans can understand, my friends were unable to give me a very accurate interpretation of the play, though sufficient to enable me to understand the plot, which in this case was as follows.

A prince was informed by his minister that in a certain far-distant town, in which was a famous shrine, there dwelt a girl of very great beauty. He decided to journey thither, ostensibly to make a pilgrimage to the shrine, but in reality to see the young woman.

She happened to be of low degree, he a prince; but, hearing that he had travelled all that distance in order to admire her beauty, she made violent love to him. He was at first unresponsive, but eventually succumbing to her charms took her away with him to his own home. His female relations, however, discovering his mésalliance, and (here is the sting) that he had paid her debts, became very angry and ill-treated the girl shamefully.

She, however, like another Griselda, submitted to all

In a Burmese Market Town

this persecution with so much sweetness and patience, that in the end even the female relations themselves were compelled to admire so much virtue, and, learning to love the girl, commended the prince's judgment, and everything ended happily.

Scenery there was none, and all the players were on the stage together, whether they were in the scene or not, those who were "unemployed" placidly smoking until they had to respond to their cues, when the cigar would be handed to another to be kept alight until their act was over. The characters in the play are generally the same—a prince, a princess, and chief clown as principals, with minor characters representing good and evil spirits, with, I think, always some representation of a dragon. The plots are generally a narrative of wrongs patiently borne by the injured lady, whose long-suffering is eventually rewarded by complete happiness. The performance itself consists largely of singing and dancing, most of which is allotted to the princess, who is often "on" for hours at a stretch. The singing is not unmusical, and the dancing very quaint, consisting largely of a slow shuffling along the stage on the flat of the foot, with an occasional backward kick with the heel. Meanwhile the arms are gesticulating in a most extraordinary manner, the play of hands and wrists being an especially noticeable point. The humour of the play naturally devolved upon the chief clown, whose remarks are, I hear, usually witty, though with the inevitable touch of immorality.

During the dialogues, as well as in song accompani-

Burma

ment, the incidental music was distinctly good I thought, and in the open air at any rate the combined tone of the orchestra was melodious.

The great attraction to me, however, lay in the character studies offered by the audience. All ages and social grades were represented. Very old people crouched over their cigars or huddled together in the cold night air, while naked babies lay in the laps of their gaily dressed mothers, who laughed and chatted with native officials or half-clad coolies. I noticed one little boy, standing bolt upright, who proved to be fast asleep, and towards midnight many of the elders also became drowsy, and would take it in turns to have a short nap, having previously arranged with their neighbours that they should be aroused when certain particularly interesting episodes occurred.

The whole scene, illuminated by the flickering light of the stage lamps and camp fires, was very fascinating, and it was some time after midnight before I could bring myself to leave it. The play, however, continued till after 2 A.M.,[1] and I learned next day that the leading lady was on the boards the whole of the time !

---

[1] These "pwes," I hear, often continue for a whole day, or even two.

CHAPTER V

I WAS very sorry to leave Taungdwingyi, where every moment of my time had been pleasantly employed, though my regret was somewhat modified by anticipations of the forest life before me, and the fact that two of my friends, Maclennan and Smythe, were to accompany me.

Leaving the bungalow at sunset, a two-hours' ride in the starlight brought us to Sathwa. The road, so called by courtesy, was terribly bad, and riding would have been difficult even by daylight, as the track (for it was little else) had been so badly cut up by cart wheels during the rains, which were only just over, that it was scored in all directions by ruts a foot or more in depth, which the sun of the last few days had baked as hard as bricks. Added to this was the fact that on either side were dense masses of jungle and forest growths, which effectually impeded what little light there was, and hid these pitfalls in an impenetrable gloom. I consider that it was more by good luck than anything else that we got through without an accident or damage to the ponies. However, we reached the dâk safely about 9 P.M., and turned in early, preparatory to our start at sunrise.

I was interested during the ride to hear our Burmese attendants singing at the pitch of their voices, an ebullition which I attributed to pure light-heartedness until I noticed that they sang *loudest* where the road was *darkest*. In reply to my inquiry, Maclennan informed me that the men were singing, "not for the fun of it," but in order to frighten away the "Nats." This superstitious feeling I found accounted for another fact which had attracted my attention. When moving, the Burmese carts are always accompanied by a horrible groaning and squeaking of the wheels ; I suggested a little grease on the axles, but learned that they preferred to have it so, as the noise, which travelled an immense distance in the still air, not only wards off the evil spirits of the forest, but also serves as a warning to their wives at home that the "master" was homeward bound, and would shortly be in want of his supper !

The dâk at Sathwa was much as others, except that the flooring boards were set so far apart that we experienced as much breeze from underneath as from the open verandah, and one had to be careful as to the position of the legs of chairs or camp bed, and as a matter of fact, while taking my bath, both sponge and soap dropped between the boards and had to be sought for below by candle-light.

The following morning elephants had arrived and were loaded up with our baggage and sent off, we following a little later on pony-back.

Jungle Life at Kokogon

A fatiguing journey through "paddy" fields, scrub jungle, and occasional forest patches, lay between us and Kokogon, in the heart of the forest itself, and to be my headquarters for the time being.

Travelling was slow and tedious owing to the absence of roads. In the cultivated lands the only pathway consisted of the tortuous little bunds or dykes which separated the irrigated patches, while in the forest dense undergrowth, largely of thorns and creepers, impeded progress and made riding difficult.

I was very much surprised at the speed with which the elephants covered the ground. Through the difficult "paddy" land they were quicker than the ponies. In some places the bunds were very narrow and slippery, while every here and there were little creeks crossed by a single log, or else by means of a ford in which the ponies floundered heavily in mud a couple of feet or more in depth, yet in every case the elephants negotiated these difficult crossings more comfortably than the ponies.

The "paddy" was ripe and harvesting in full operation. The Burmans use sickles for reaping, cutting the straw half-way up so as to gather some and yet leave enough for the cattle in the fields to browse upon. The rice is bound into sheaves with a "strap," as at home, and is later on carted to the "talin" or threshing-floor, where, in the usual Eastern manner, the grain is trodden out by bullocks. Winnowing is performed by means of a circular tray, about two feet in diameter, which is tossed into the air with a rotary motion, so as to set all its contents spinning, the chaff being blown away while the grain falls at the operator's feet.

At every halt innumerable claims were presented by the villagers for the value of the rice consumed by the elephants on the road. In most cases these claims were for quantities far beyond the animals' power of consumption, and after a little good-humoured badinage, were easily compounded for half the original sum demanded. In one case, however, the native appeared to be quite clear as to the justice of his claim, and, scouting the idea of any compromise, exclaimed, "You may cut my throat if I am telling a lie!"

His claim was paid in full, and I noticed that in all their dealings with them the employees of the Corporation gave the natives the benefit of the doubt, and no matter at what cost made it a matter of principle to keep faith with them.

That such an attitude is honourable and wise goes without saying, and it has its reward in the friendly relationship existing between the "jungle wallah" and his subordinates. I one day heard a native remark to a stranger, "We *have* to shikoh to the Government official who eats our money, but we like to shikoh to the Bombay-Burma Thakins whose money we eat," and I may say that, during the weeks I spent in riding through the forest I had frequent demonstrations of the esteem and respect in which the Corporation and their agents were held by natives of all classes.

The country through which we had passed was

Jungle Life at Kokogon

extremely pretty in its general effect,—immense tracts of "paddy" land, interspersed with trees, among which were the villages of the peasants, in many cases surrounded by groves of bananas and other fruit-trees, while large pools, overgrown with lotus, were a common feature.

The moisture in the saturated land, sucked up by the powerful sun, filled the air with an impalpable mist which enveloped the landscape in a silver haze, and gave to its features a suggestiveness which was charming. Distances which were not really great appeared to be immense, and the sun, shining through the laden atmosphere, glorified even the monotony of the rice-fields with opalescent tints, amidst which the brightly coloured costumes of the natives shone like jewels. This silvery curtain, which lends such enchantment to the commonplace, I found to be general in the cultivated lands, and during the few hours of its continuance it seems to envelop nature in a poetic glamour difficult to describe.

Our entrance into the forest was almost abrupt, the "paddy" land being succeeded by patches of kaing grass, bamboo, and a tangled growth of all kinds, glittering under the hot sun, which caused the steam to rise from the pools and damp patches of the paths well into the day. Some of the vistas were very lovely, the nearer points standing out strongly against a distance hazy in the hot air, through which our elephants loomed large and almost phantom-like.

Huge trees of to me as yet strange growths towered

Burma

above the undergrowth, their individual characteristics being largely lost in the profusion of creepers which enveloped them in a uniform habit of leaves and flowers, and whose sinuous stems winding through the grasses tripped up our ponies and rendered riding slow and difficult. Evidently the haunt of game, all we saw on this march were a few "gyi" or barking deer, which dashed across our path, though this forest abounds with tiger, panther, and elephant, while everywhere among the succulent undergrowth were signs of large herds of "pig."

Birds there were in plenty, minahs, hoopoe, king crow, jungle fowl and owls, also a large number of paddy birds, the female of which, I noticed, is not white but parti-coloured, brown predominating, which makes her very difficult to find when nesting. Doves were cooing, and in the nyoung-bin trees the green pigeon was whistling a melody which Skeene once declared to be a few bars from *The Belle of New York*! There is one bird, however, which I have met with in different parts of Burma, but whose species I have never been able to discover, whose song consists of a distinct musical phrase of several bars. He is a small bird, with a liquid note, rich and full, and his song sounds gloriously beautiful in the often solemn surroundings of the forest.

Squirrels were there in large numbers, disputing with the monkeys for possession of the nut-trees, while flitting across the glades flights of parrots flashed brilliant in the sunlight.

Jungle Life at Kokogon

That wild animals always look their best in their natural environment is a truism which certainly applies strongly to the parrot. Seen at home as a caged bird he has little beauty, and might almost be described as a grotesque. Here, however, in these primeval forests, he is a creature of beauty and joy. Hear him whistling softly to his mate, or exchanging calls with his fellows as he sits in the topmost bough of a cotton-tree, 200 feet above ground. Every note is flute-like and coaxing, and, as his song floats downwards towards you through the sun-bathed air, each note is mellowed and sweetened on its journey. Or again, as a flock suddenly launches itself into space, and plays "follow my leader" through the tree-tops, what could be prettier than they as their orange beaks and long slender tails glint in the sunlight! It is a revel of song and colour and pure light-heartedness foreign to their caged and subdued relatives in this country. Here a parrot is simply a curiosity, there a beautiful creature, suited to its surroundings, and bringing an air of gladness and colour into what might otherwise have been an oppressive exuberance of forest growth.

Curiously enough, there were few insects; no doubt as the heat was intense they were lying dormant in the leafy shades. Butterflies, however, were plentiful and of great beauty.

I am afraid my recollection of this part of my journey is not very definite. Being my first introduction to virgin forest, I found it all so strange that I was content to wonder at its confused beauty and luxuriance without attempting to make notes, mental or otherwise; much of our attention, moreover, had to be directed to the order of our going.

Travelling in the paddy land had been difficult. Here, however, it was more so; the open glades were often marshy, and under the powerful sun were giving up steam as late as mid-day. Riding through the thickets was almost impossible on account of the hidden creepers which made it difficult for the pony to travel, and the thorns which lacerated the rider and the beast indiscriminately, so that of two evils it was usually better to stick to the open and be grilled, than risk the difficulties and perhaps dangers of the denser forest.

Few signs of human life disturbed the solitude of these wilds. Here and there were little clearings planted in rice or sessamine, over which grotesque scarecrows stood sentinel, or perhaps an occasional hut of bamboo and grasses marked the halting-place of previous travellers; and once I saw a boy engaged in snaring wild-fowl by the aid of a decoy cock, the *modus operandi* apparently being to tether the bird in a patch of short grass, where he is surrounded by a circle of snares composed of twigs, and the forest bird, responding to his challenge, comes down to fight him and is caught.

Kokogon was reached at 1 P.M., and I must confess that I promptly went to sleep in a chair after tiffin. Burma is a sleepy country, and the siesta a general institution for both man and beast, and I always found it difficult to resist the inclination to sleep in the early

Jungle Life at Kokogon

afternoon. It was only by recommencing my work directly after lunch that I was able to overcome this feeling of drowsiness, which, however, on one or two occasions completely mastered me.

Kokogon is practically the centre of a large teak forest, which was being worked by the Corporation. Their bungalow, which is some little distance from the native village, was pleasantly situated in an island of grass surrounded by dense forest and jungle, and overlooking the Kyouk-mee-choung, a forest creek or river, where a number of elephants were at work clearing a "pone" of logs brought down by the last freshet.

Behind the bungalow were storehouses, stables, and the huts of the woodmen, among which moved the wives and children of the foresters bringing in sticks, and kindling fires preparatory to cooking the evening meal. Below us, in the shade of the bungalow, our ponies were being attended to and the baggage unloaded from the elephants.

Later in the afternoon all the elephants at work in the creek, twelve in all with three calves, came in for their evening feed : a picturesque sight, as each, mounted by its "oozi,"[1] came to the steps of the bungalow to "salaam," and perhaps receive a "tit-bit," before proceeding to the lines where rows of buckets containing rice are waiting ready for them. After feeding, the elephants go down to the creek to bathe before being turned into the jungle for the night. Very pretty was

[1] Driver.

the scene, as the declining sun caught the red cliffs which formed the river's banks, and lit up the mixed foliage of the forest with a ruddy light, to which the deep gloom of the shades offered a striking contrast. As the sun, red and glorious, slowly disappeared behind the trees, crickets and frogs began their evensong, while in the distance the trumpeting of an elephant, or the impatient squeal of a calf which had temporarily lost its mother, were the only sounds to break the solemn hush which comes over the forest at sun-down. Presently, as the evening breeze rustled through the tree-tops, the cry of the jackal and hoot of the owl broke the stillness, and the rising moon completed the poetic feeling of a scene which combined so much of suggestion with its solemn beauty.

Altogether the day's experience had been of extreme if somewhat bewildering interest. Many sharp contrasts had presented themselves on the way, culminating in this rich forest scenery, which as yet I had hardly begun to understand, so entirely different was it from anything I had hitherto seen. Beautiful but impressive, solitary yet alive, I felt that I must discover many of its secrets before I could hope to fully appreciate its fascination myself or pen an adequate description for my friends.

Darkness drove me back to the bungalow, where dinner awaited three hungry men, and a runner was preparing to start back upon his two-days' journey through the jungle, to post our letters at Taung-dwingyi.

Jungle Life at Kokogon

I am often asked how we fared in the jungle. Here is our menu for this first night :—

Mulligatawny soup.	Roast chicken, bread sauce
Cod's roe.	and crumbs.
Fricassee of chicken.	Curry and rice.
Steak and onions, and	Cold York ham.
potatoes.	Carlsbad plums.
Chip potatoes.	

We had also bread, and butter in tins (usually in a liquid state, however), and though as we travelled farther fresh provisions gave out, the thoughtfulness displayed by my friends in selecting stores, and the cleverness of our servants in contriving, provided meals as varied and generally as palatable as this one, jungle fowl or deer taking the place of chicken, and biscuits that of bread. Vegetables became a difficulty, however, for though the villagers would bring presents of fruit and eggs, we seldom got anything in the shape of green food.

While we were at dinner the men had brought in several elephant-loads of logs and lit a huge bonfire in front of the verandah, and as the nights are cold we gathered round it gratefully. In its fitful light, and surrounded by the blackness of the forest, I took my first hand at bridge, but as there were only three of us, and none of us was quite sure of the rules applying to perpetual dummy, the game became a little confused, though it served to pass the evening very happily till our early bedtime.

The first flush of dawn found us up and preparing

for our day's work, the suddenness and extraordinary glory of the sunrise as it almost instantly suffused the sky explaining the apparent incongruity of Kipling's line, " the dawn comes up like thunder," which I now see to aptly describe a phenomenon which is almost startling. Half an hour later every one was at work, I at my painting, the elephants and jungle wallahs with their logs.

Without wishing to attempt a long dissertation upon teak-growing or forestry generally, it will, I think, be of interest if I give a short description of the nature of the work upon which so many of our young men are engaged in the forests of Burma.

As is perhaps generally known, teak, pyingado (iron-wood tree), and several other species are " protected " by the Government, their extraction being sanctioned under certain well-defined rules. Pyingado is too heavy to be profitably worked except locally for the purpose of railway sleepers, and the attention of the great firms is entirely devoted to the extraction of teak, licenses for which are granted, and zones or "forests" allotted to them in consideration of the rather heavy royalties charged upon the logs marketed. Each of these forests is managed by a representative of the firm concerned, assisted by several subordinates who supervise the work being carried on ; the selection of trees to be felled, however, rests entirely with the Government forest officer, and is made with proper regard to the replenishment of the forests under his control.

The trees selected are " girdled " by cutting a ring

LOADING TEAK AT KOKOGON

through the bark and sapwood until the hard wood is entered, the result being that, cut off from any supply of moisture from the roots, the tree dies, and the bark, leaves, and twigs having fallen off, the naturally seasoned tree is felled at from two to three years after girdling. The trees are reckoned first or second class trees according to their size, the former being from 6 to 7 feet and the latter about $4\frac{1}{2}$ feet in girth, their ages varying from 35 to 120 years, I believe. The teak is a handsome tree, straight-stemmed, as a rule, branching much like an acacia at about 25 or 30 feet from the ground. Its leaves are very large, shaped like an elm but smoother, and they have a purple blossom which stands up from among the foliage, remaining on the tree for a considerable time after the leaf has fallen.

After felling, the difficult work of transport begins. In many cases the logs lie in inaccessible parts of the forest, which necessitates the making of roads and building of bridges before the work of hauling can be commenced. Large numbers of elephants and bullocks are engaged in this work, and in one place at least the Corporation have a traction engine at work. In this process of transportation the forest rivers or creeks are used to the utmost, until finally some large water-way is reached by means of which the rafted logs may be floated down to the sea.[1]

[1] I hope I am not exaggerating, but my recollection is that often as long a period as nine, or in some cases even twelve years elapses between the girdling of a tree and its final arrival at the sawmills at Rangoon.

Burma

These creeks seem to be more or less of the same character. Though there is always a little water flowing in the bed, it is only after rain that they can claim any title to be called rivers. Owing to the steepness of the watershed and the extraordinary amount of rainfall when it occurs, what before was a sleepy succession of pools, half stagnating in the sun, becomes almost immediately a rushing, swirling river, carrying with it tree-trunks and all kinds of forest débris. These floods are the opportunity for the "jungle wallah," who has been busily employed in teak felling and hauling in readiness for a rise. All hands are busily engaged in launching logs into the stream, along whose banks are stationed parties of men and elephants shoving off logs should they strand, and with almost superhuman effort and at considerable risk of life relieving a "jam," which is often caused by the falling of a forest tree where the flood has undermined the bank. It is a time of high pressure and strenuous effort on the part of all engaged in the work, for these streams form the easiest, sometimes the only, means of transit, and a freshet when it occurs must be utilised to its fullest advantage. I am told that it is not infrequent for men engaged in the teak forest to be out for two or three days continuously, the whole time working night and day under the extremest physical discomfort caused by drenching rain and smothering mud, unable for a moment to relax the closest concentration upon work which demands the maximum of physical endurance, resourcefulness, and pluck. The

Jungle Life at Kokogon

river falls as quickly as it rises, and leaves the logs committed to its charge stranded in piles called "pones," or perhaps in single logs dotted here and there throughout its course. These pones are usually formed by an obstruction, such as an impeding rock, or where a log sticks upright in the muddy bed. In some cases, however, the logs are collected into a "pone" by means of a boom placed across the creek to prevent them going farther down stream. This boom is called "thittagah," which means literally "a door for logs." Such a place was Kokogon, where the elephants were engaged in hauling the collected timber up a slide of rollers on to the high bank, from where it will presently be hauled through the forest by bullock waggon or traction engine to another and a larger stream, which will float it down to Rangoon.

Apropos of this, one of my companions had a somewhat curious adventure while engaged on the work which I have been describing. He was making his way down the creek, finding such foothold as he could, and presently stood upon what he took to be the root of a tree lying on the face of the steep bank. He was much alarmed to find it move and to witness the erection of an enormous neck and head at the end farthest from him. What he had taken for a twisted tree-stem proved to be a 13-foot python, and, as he told me, he "let off a yell" and both barrels of the gun which he happened to be carrying as he jumped for the river bed. Luckily the python was killed, and he took the skin, of which he is very proud.

Burma

I have previously remarked upon my not having seen a snake so far, but closely following upon the above adventure, one morning in going to my work I trod upon a cobra, which fortunately was more alarmed than myself and darted off at amazing speed into the thicket; and the same evening one of our party in feeding the camp fire, picked up what he thought to be a chip, but which was nothing less than a Russell's viper, one of the most deadly snakes of Burma. Fortunately he had "caught it right," and dropped it before any harm was done.

With regard to snakes generally, I think it is unquestioned that the reptile is, in most instances, as anxious to get out of the way as the human being to avoid it. An exception, however, occurs in the case of the hamadryad or king cobra, which is aggressive. A friend of mine in the Katha district told me how, when chased by one of them, he, though an extremely athletic man, had the greatest difficulty in getting away, so rapid was its movement, and it was only by throwing down his gun and cartridge-bag that he was able to outdistance his pursuer.

It is interesting to watch the elephants at work; their sagacity is remarkable, and they hardly seem to require the direction of the "oozis" who sit astride their necks, encouraging them with cries of "kolai" (brother), or repressing the refractory ones with their "choons." [1] In order to assist his driver to mount, an elephant will either kneel, or by bending the fore-leg,

[1] Driving hooks.

upon which the "oozi" steps, lift him until his seat is reached. The prettiest method, perhaps, is when the elephant, bending the head, curls up his trunk, which, together with his broad forehead, forms a simple and easy staircase for its driver. Approaching a log the elephant will look at it and touch it deprecatingly with his trunk, and, having mentally decided as to its probable weight, will either lift it as directed, or should he consider it too heavy, will positively decline to touch it unassisted. Very clever, too, is the manner in which they avoid obstacles, stepping over logs, chains, etc., as they go about their work. In lifting timber, both trunk and tusks are used, and it is extraordinary how they marshal and sort the logs, laying them neatly and evenly in their places, shoving with the head and rolling them over until arranged to their satisfaction ; or, when loading the trolleys, how carefully the log is laid down, and then pushed forwards or backwards until a perfect balance is obtained.

Highly intelligent animals, they are apparently docile also, except when the male goes "must," or in the case of a female with a calf. Then either is a very uncertain quantity ; the calves also are most pugnacious, even vicious, and as even a "youngster" will weigh close upon half a ton, and is quite able to squash the life out of any one, they are not to be trifled with by any means.

I was one day taking a photograph of the elephants at work at the top of the slide by which the logs were hauled from the river to the top of the bank. Wishing

Burma

to get a good one, I was focussing carefully on the screen, my head being under the cloth; suddenly I noticed one of the elephants becoming very rapidly larger, and at the same time heard shouts of "Look out!" Without waiting to see what was going on, however, I snatched up my camera and dropped over the steep bank into the river bed below. I then discovered that I had been charged by one of these fond mothers, and had narrowly escaped a serious danger. The elephant in question, I afterwards learnt, had previously killed two of her "oozis," and was altogether a lady to be avoided.

Generally speaking, a great attachment springs up between the elephant and his driver, who is often devoted to his charge. I heard of a case where an employer, on transferring his elephants to a new district, asked one of the drivers to leave his village and come also. "Of course," he replied, "how can I leave my elephant; he is my father, with whom I have worked thirteen years."

On the other hand, elephants have a strong objection to ponies and Europeans, especially when approached from behind. Several times in moving through the forest I came upon our "travellers" unexpectedly, and in every case the elephant, striking his trunk upon the ground, and giving a shrill metallic cry, quite different from his ordinary trumpeting, would turn round to attack. My pony, however, was always ready, and quickly carried me out of sight among the trees.

I was rather surprised to learn how tender are

elephants' backs, and the greatest care must be exercised in loading up a "traveller" to ensure a perfect balance of the load, or a sore back is sure to result. Curiously enough also, they suffer a good deal from the bites of mosquitoes and other stinging insects, and I have, on several occasions, seen the blood trickling down their corrugated and seemingly impenetrable hides from this cause.

CHAPTER VI

THROUGH THE FOREST TO PYINMANA

DURING the time spent at Kokogon, I was able to familiarise myself with many forest growths, but when it is considered that there are in Burma over 1500 different species of trees alone, without regarding the lesser growths, my little knowledge was after all but a qualified ignorance, though sufficient to add greatly to the pleasure of the succeeding weeks spent in other parts of the forest.

As usual our day's march began at dawn, and owing to the difficulty of travelling through the denser portions of the forest, often continued until nightfall.

The early mornings were peculiarly lovely, fresh, even cold, with the dew hanging heavy upon spikes of grass and other vegetation, and spangling the huge cobwebs which hid among them with a weight of water I hardly thought them capable of sustaining. As we rode through the kaing grass and longer reeds, their dripping heads gave us a veritable shower-bath, and in a very short time every one was wet through.

The days were hot, the sun having a peculiar

potency from which even solar topees were hardly a protection, and even the weight of silk suits seemed insufferable.

Towards evening, as the air cooled and the brassy sky became soft with mellow tints, our surroundings were increasingly beautiful. Instead of the hard glitter of light on trunks and boughs, which seemed coldly white against the blackness of the shades, all the lovely tints and variations of foliage and flowers are properly appreciated.

Out of a tangled mass of creepers, palms, begonias, lilies, and a variety of other growths, spring huge cotton-trees whose straight white trunks rise 100 feet or more into the air before branching into the splendid crests they carry, the pyingado, almost as high, the large-leaved teak, banyan, cutch, and indaing trees being all more or less bound together by fantastic creepers, whose tendrils droop gracefully from boughs further enriched by huge growths of orchids.

Many of the flowering plants are very lovely, including several varieties of convolvulus, blue, yellow, and white with a deep mauve centre, many of the canariensis kind, and the particularly beautiful scarlet tropæolum. These entirely envelop the smaller jungle trees, forming natural arbours, which look as though they had been carefully planted and tended by gardeners.

During the day these wilds are gay with birds and the thickets are alive with game. Towards evening insect life awakes, and the shrill note of the crickets is a perpetual accompaniment to the dance of the fireflies.

Burma

Personally I was not troubled by insects ; mosquitoes are, of course, plentiful, but they did not seem to me to be as malicious as their town cousins. With regard to the others they were more interesting than irritating, the spiders and ants alone being a source of annoyance.

The sounds of the forest are peculiar, for in addition to the gentle swish of the breeze through the boughs is the "pap-pap" of the larger leaves, and the rattle of dry bean pods as they swing, or fall from bough to bough to the undergrowth below. The rapping of woodpeckers also mingles with the croaking of tree frogs or the screech of owl or squirrel. It is all very weird, and at night to these noises are added the cry of the panther and jackal, and the shrill trumpeting of elephants.

Here and there through the forest are the graves of woodmen, marked by a little fence of twigs or a covering of basket-work,—solemn resting-places, whose simple adornment is compensated by the magnificent dignity of the trees which overshadow them. At intervals are the "nat-sin" or rest-houses and pagodas of wicker-work erected by the superstitious natives in order to propitiate the spirits of the forest, in many of which are placed diminutive utensils and weapons, and offerings of food.

Giant ant-hills are frequent, and are in some instances 9 feet or more in height, but of all the curiosities of the forest the creepers interested me most. How they reach their position is often a puzzle. I noticed one of perhaps 12 or 15 inches diameter, which sprang

Through the Forest to Pyinmana

from the root of one tree, and in one single shoot had crossed a glade of perhaps 30 yards and attached itself to the top of a tree 50 feet in height, thus forming an entirely unsupported aerial bridge.

Another curious growth, which at first I mistook for a creeper, is the *Ficus religiosa* or sacred banyan, more generally spoken of in Burma as the "nyaung-bin," the home of the green pigeon, who feeds upon its berries. Sometimes the seed has been dropped by a bird into the fork of a tree where, taking root, it sends down shoots which cling closely to the trunk until the earth is reached. From this moment these roots, as they really are, commence to grow upwards, and, swelling as they grow, develop into enormous encircling arms strongly resembling the tentacles of an octopus, while from above corresponding boughs mix their foliage with that of the parent tree. By degrees the original tree is entirely enveloped in an outer casing of ficus, which slowly crushes the life out of the enclosed trunk, and from its starting-point, perhaps 100 feet above ground, rears its crest as a new tree, even larger than the one which at first gave it support. In one particular case I saw that two neighbouring trees had been enveloped in this way, presenting the singular phenomenon of three distinct kinds of foliage springing from what appeared to be a single trunk.

When the forest indulges in freaks of this kind it is perhaps not surprising that the average "jungle wallah" gives up the puzzle! He knows his teak, pyingado, eng, and cutch, and perhaps a few others whose economic properties render them of value, but the rest he is content to regard as "jungle wood" and nothing more.

Generally speaking, the forest consists of three tiers of growth, the lower consisting of scrub, grasses, bamboo, and a few small trees. Above these rise the teak, cutch, cinnamon, palms, and a few others, which are again dominated by a tier of giants, straight in the trunk and immensely tall, as though sucked up by the damp heat, the most imposing of these being the cotton-tree, whose 200 feet of trunk and crest is supported at the base by enormous buttresses, without which its spongy texture could hardly withstand the pressure of the wind. These larger trunks are generally smooth-skinned, though in many cases the bark is broken by spiral corrugations, which I observed most frequently turned in the direction of the sun's course.

As a rule, the trees are either large-leaved or feathery in their foliage. Among the first are the banyan, of which there are several varieties, teak, rubber, indaing and a variety of broad-leaved palms, while of the latter are pepper, padouk, tamarind, cutch, and several other varieties of acacia. A great many of them bear thorns, particularly the feathery species.

I often found it difficult in the deep forest to identify the foliage of any given tree, the boughs being so much intermingled, and their own foliage in many cases being so completely smothered in an enormous mass of leaf and flower of the seemingly endless variety of creepers. Orchids appear to grow on all the lofty trees, some bunches being large enough to fill a small cart could they be removed. Many of the forest trees flower, such as the " flame of the forest," padouk, cotton-tree, dhak, pepper, and gold mohur. Among the palms are cocoa-nut, toddy, palmyra, and areca-nut, while the lesser growths include the castor-oil, with its fleshy leaf, tree potato, plantains of many varieties, and a great many species of bamboo. I noticed many dwarf wild dates among the undergrowth, but, as one of my companions informed me, " there were no *tame* dates in the country"! In many districts were wild pineapples, and occasionally the papaya, with its delicious fruit, from the seeds of which pepsine is made. One thing that struck me as curious in so damp a country was the almost total absence of ferns or fungi, though I later on saw many varieties of both in the forests of the Northern Shan States.

Such is a general impression of the forest through which I was travelling, but as the ground was varied by steep undulations, often rising to a considerable height, the character of its trees and growth varied considerably according to the levels.

On leaving Kokogon the first part of our journey was through forest of the rich character I have described. Crossing the creek our track lay through the teak forest, where in an open glade I had my last glimpse of elephants at work loading the logs on to trolleys, behind them rising a splendid cotton-tree smothered in creepers, and entirely dwarfing the teak and other trees which surrounded it.

Burma

The "road," so called, was only a partly defined track, often entirely overgrown with grasses and obstructed by fallen timber and clinging vines. The ground was generally sandy, but here and there were "pockets" of clay which had not yet dried up, and were simply traps for the unwary. As our elephants had been sent on ahead, their heavy footprints, two feet in depth, furnished what I may call "stepping-stones" across the worst places, the ponies jumping from one to the other very cleverly, and so effecting a crossing where otherwise they might have been bogged. In other places the track ran up steep hill-sides, and consisted merely of a rut full of mud held up by the roots which traversed it, so forming an irregular kind of staircase up which our ponies had to clamber as best they could. As in many cases these "steps" were four feet or so in height, our ponies constantly slipped back upon their haunches, rendering riding extremely difficult, more especially as the path was further obstructed by stumps of jungle wood, which might well have caused damage to horse or rider.

Crossing a ridge of laterite, the forest consisted entirely of in or eng trees, much like the Spanish oak in appearance ; here there was little scrub, the undergrowth consisting almost entirely of lesser grasses and a few flowering plants. Descending the slope, this dry forest was succeeded by a beautiful wood, green and shady, in which were many of our own wood plants mixed with strange flowers, and which, with an occasional cotton-tree or pyingado, gave the only tropical feature

Through the Forest to Pyinmana

to scenery which otherwise closely resembled an English coppice.

Then almost suddenly we entered what might literally be described as a botanic garden. On either side of the road, here well defined, were flowers of various kinds,—blue, yellow, white, red, all growing together on a tangled mass of greenery. The lesser trees were almost covered with climbing plants, while from the highest hung festoons of creepers like garlands of green and gold. Flitting across the patches of sunlight were plumage birds, while flights of peacocks moved heavily from tree to tree.

This again was succeeded by a bamboo forest, most beautiful of all,—vista after vista, like cathedral aisles, arched by the feathery boughs of the bamboos, which sprang from a floor of almost white sand. Very solemn it was in the subdued light, for little sunlight was able to penetrate through the green vault, and the very air seemed cold and awed. Down in the deeper hollows was blackness; up the slopes a kind of artificial half-light pervaded the network of intersecting bamboo stems, and in some places, where the foliage was a little thinner, lilies carpeted the ground. I find it impossible to describe the beauty of it all, especially where it was reflected in a forest stream, which added its quota of water plants to the already luxuriant foliage.

Water erosion hereabouts is heavy, and results in practically all the roads and bridges being carried away each monsoon, entailing a great amount of work upon the forest men to make good the damage.

95

Burma

The forest is at its best during the rains. Trees and orchids are in bloom, and birds and butterflies more in evidence; while the atmospheric effects, particularly at sunset, are more striking and gorgeous in colour than at any other time of the year. Insect life, however, is apt to be inconvenient at this season, lamps and candles are put out by the white ants, while an infinite variety of flying insects render indoor life well-nigh intolerable. In the forest the roads become rivers of mud, impassable for ponies, and in which pedestrians often sink above the waist. This is a trying time for the forest men, for whom an added terror exists in the large numbers of leeches with which the mud is permeated, some of them being so small as to get through the eyelet-holes of one's boots, and producing irritating wounds in addition to the mud sores common to the season.

We camped that night at a place called Hlai-bindoung, in a small "tai" or rest-house, which consisted of three walls of bamboo matting, thatched with "thekke," and as usual raised on piles, the front of the house being entirely open to the air.

We were in rather a dense forest, composed largely of bamboo, with a pretty little stream winding through the undergrowth before us. A "snaky" place, however, and I felt it necessary to station my servant behind me with a stick while I was painting in the adjacent jungle.

At nightfall the usual log fire was lit, around which we had our evening meal. Everything had been strange to me during the day's ride, and even the flames of our fire had a peculiarity of their own, rising in long slender tongues to a great height, and without the splutter and noise usually associated with a wood fire. Meanwhile from the forest came sounds like shot-guns being fired, but which I learned were simply caused by our elephants pulling down the bamboos in order to feed upon their green shoots, the hollow stems "going off" like pop-guns as they broke.

Like the cattle the elephants wear a "kalouk," composed of a circular drum of teak-wood, hollowed through its entire length, with two hardwood clappers suspended on the outside by a cord which runs through the clappers and bell, and is tied round the elephant's neck. As the elephants are always turned loose at night to forage for themselves, it is only by means of the kalouk that the oozi is able to locate and capture his animal in the jungle. I am told that each driver recognises the tone of the bell his elephant wears, so that he never makes the mistake of hunting down the wrong animal. These elephant bells also serve the purpose of warding off bears, tigers, and other marauders at night. So useful in this way is the kalouk that I heard of one case where an isolated camp had been repeatedly attacked by bears, which were with some difficulty driven off, and the servants eventually adopted the habit of carrying one in their hands, which so alarmed the bears by the supposed presence of elephants that they retired from the vicinity of the camp altogether.

Burma

I do not think I ever experienced cold to equal that of my first night in a forest "tai." As I have already explained, one side of the building is entirely open to the air, while matting walls afford little protection against the wind; one naturally, therefore, "turned in" in flannels with all available blankets on the bed. Sleep proved impossible, the cold was so intense; and presently I was compelled to get up, add more clothing to what I already wore, and put my topcoat and anything in the shape of packing canvases I could find on top of the blankets, but without result. Eventually I came to the conclusion that the cold was caused by the damp exhalations from the ground, so, reversing the order of things, I placed my heavy bedding underneath me, simply wrapping myself in my ulster, after which, although I still felt the cold intensely, I was able to sleep.

At about 4.30 A.M. I was awakened by what I at first thought was a downpour of rain, but which proved to be nothing else than the heavy dew, which, collecting on the large leaves, dripped from one to the other like a thunder-shower, and was of sufficient volume to flow from the eaves of the rest-house in a continual stream.[1]

This district is very rich in game, and we found traces of sambur, gyi, leopard, tiger, and wild elephant here, also many signs of pig. Among the feathered game were jungle fowl, pheasant, partridge, wood-

---

[1] This period of heavy dew-fall lasts about two and a half months, the "hot" weather commencing about the 15th of February, followed later by the monsoon rains.

pigeon, wild duck, snipe, and peacock, the latter being very good eating.

One of my friends in following up the track of a pig here eventually lost the trail in a thicket of kaing grass, so he sent his servant round it to see if the tracks came through, or if the quarry were asleep in the grass. On reaching the other side the man found a panther asleep, and, without disturbing him, came and informed his master, who promptly went in search of the bigger game. The pig, however, was now aroused and alarmed the panther just as my friend came up, and, both breaking simultaneously in opposite directions, he failed to bag either. This, with the exception of a few gyi, was all we ourselves saw in the way of game hereabouts.

All through this ride, my pony, a four-year-old, exhibited great signs of nervousness, and I had often considerable difficulty in keeping him in hand. It was his first experience of the forest, the gloom and stillness of which were so great that the breaking of a twig served to alarm him. He continually shied at roots or branches on the ground, and was perpetually sniffing the air or snorting at imaginary terrors. Possibly he smelt tiger or feared snakes, but whatever the cause, on one or two occasions he incontinently bolted, crashing through thorns and creepers and jamming me against tree-trunks in his flight. Twice I completely lost the track, but knowing the general direction of our march I was each time able to pick up the elephant-treads again and rejoin my party. The sensation of being lost, however, is not pleasant, particularly in a jungle frequented by tiger—the more so as I was entirely unarmed.

One of my friends told me how, after a similar experience, he was obliged to sleep in the open all night, and next day found himself only a mile from his camp, which through the density of the growth he had been unable to find. Fortunately he had a gun with him, and a jungle fowl supplied his evening meal, without which he would have been obliged to pass the night fasting.

Such few natives as inhabit these forests are mostly Chins, whose villages are picturesquely placed in a clearing surmounting a hillock, and surrounded by the usual stockade. The dwellings and costumes of the inhabitants are poorer than those of their Burmese neighbours, and to judge by the limited area of cultivation in the vicinity of their hamlets, they would appear to live largely upon the forest.

In features they are uncomely, and they have the curious custom of still further disfiguring their women by tattooing their faces black all over immediately after marriage. This is done in order to limit the probability of other men running after their wives, and I can hardly doubt that it has the desired effect. All the older women I saw were so treated, but the younger ones are rebelling against the custom, which in many districts is beginning to die out.

Though varying from time to time in particular features, one day's journey through the forest was much

DAWN IN THE FOREST

like another. Surrounded by scenes of the supremest beauty, each day's ride seemed more beautiful than the last,—a gradual crescendo of loveliness which only increased as familiarity aided appreciation, and of which no words of mine could ever give an adequate impression. I had never anticipated anything so completely fascinating as these Burmese forests proved to be, and my lasting regret is that, owing to the difficulties of the way and the impossibility of keeping in touch with my baggage, I was unable to secure as many pictures as I could have wished with which to supplement my descriptions.

At our halting-places at night an additional touch of romance was given by the flickering light of the camp fires illuminating forest trees and the figures of those who sat around them. Here, after a hard day's ride and a well-earned meal, I was glad to lie in its warmth, acquiring information from my companions, or listening to their anecdotes and tales of adventure in other parts of the country, while from the blackness of the gloom beyond came sounds which warned the traveller that a new life had awakened in the forest, the investigation of which it would be unwise to attempt.

On December 13 and 14 I was camped at Delanchoon, where I was for the first time partially incapacitated by fever, from which hitherto I had been remarkably free. The tai here is a Government one, and better built than the others in which I had stayed, and the additional comfort of which I appreciated under the circumstances, but unfortunately I was not able to work much here, as I spent most of my time in the shelter of the house. This being a good opportunity, I took a photograph of my friends and the whole of our servants, and, as it happened, it proved my last chance of doing so. In marshalling the men I was amused by a little altercation between two of them. One was heard to say, "What nonsense is this, I am not going to be photographed," to which the other replied, "How can it be nonsense when 'Master' want it !" and in due course he took his place with the rest.

Near by was a small village, and the natives as usual brought presents of fruit, etc., and among other items a lemur which they had caught on the way. As they are pretty little beasts, easily tamed and quickly becoming attached to their master, I would have liked to have brought this one home with me, but the difficulties were too great, and it was eventually sent to the little monastery attached to the village.

Here also I saw a herd of wild elephants browsing among the bamboos, but owing to the thickness of the jungle I was not able to obtain any studies of them, and it would have been most unwise to have attempted too near an approach for the purpose. As an example of the dangers of elephant-stalking I may mention the case of a servant of the Corporation who, riding a tame elephant, was with others engaged in rounding up a wild herd in the Katha district. A bull broke from the herd, and charging the ring which hemmed him in, so alarmed the elephant which our friend was riding that it turned and bolted, passing under a heavy bough which swept him off its back to the ground, where he lay with several bones broken, unable to move. He was then seized by the elephant's trunk and tossed into the air again and again, alternately crashing against the limbs of overhanging trees, or falling heavily to the earth, until he lay a bruised and broken mass, and practically lifeless. Not content with this, the bull finally lowered his head and charged his victim, but, marvellous to relate, though the elephant's tusks ploughed up deep furrows on either side of him, he was untouched by either feet or tusks, and the elephant then making off he was rescued by his friends. It seems hardly credible that he could have survived, but when I left Burma I learned that he had made considerable progress towards complete recovery.

Our next halting-place was Min-byin, the day's ride being peculiarly interesting. At first our path lay through a mixed forest of lofty trees and giant bamboo sixty feet in height. The ground was very hilly, affording alternate vistas of dark alleys of greenery interspersed with flowers, or from the hill-tops, over feathery foliage to a succession of more distant ridges. The particular charm of the ride, however, lay in the fact that for the greater part of the way we followed the windings of the Min-byin river, in which all this wealth of tropical foliage was reflected. These riparian forests are peculiarly rich, the usual growths being supplemented by many water-side plants not found on the higher levels, the foliage of which is naturally particularly fresh in colour. Owing to the steepness

of the hills and the unusual density of the undergrowth we presently took to the river, riding through
the shallow water, which was seldom more than a foot
in depth. These partially dry streams often form the
best road for riding or walking, and from the tracks in
the sandy bed the Min-byin river was evidently a highway for carts also.

Our course was generally southerly, and the scene
was extremely pretty as our trailing caravan wound
along the creek, the figures standing out strongly
against the water shimmering in the sunshine. Some
of the bends in the river were very fine. From the
farther side the forest rose in hills of deepest shade,
only the edges of the trees catching the brilliant light,
while from the nearer bank a spit of white sand edged
with a silver streak glittered in contrast with the
gloom beyond. Kingfishers flitted from bank to bank,
and an occasional grey heron flew heavily away as we
approached. Birds of many kinds added their brilliant
colouring to that of the flowers which shone among
the varied greens, while all the forest trees were full
of character.

This part of my journey formed the climax to a
succession of beautiful scenes, and nowhere had I seen
flowers so varied or in such profusion as here.

An amusing episode occurred during this march.
I was as usual loitering while adding pages to my
sketch-book, and became separated from my party, and
presently happened upon a native who was using a
curious two-stringed bow, with which he shot clay

bullets instead of arrows. I endeavoured to make him understand that I wished to buy the weapon, but unsuccessfully ; so, rather than lose the opportunity of securing such an interesting curio, I annexed the bow, and made him follow me to Min-byin, where my friends could interpret for me. I was rather disconcerted to find that the man had no desire to part with the bow, as well as concerned at having brought him, practically a prisoner, so far out of his way. I asked Maclennan what I should do. " Oh, keep the bow and give him two rupees and send him away," he advised. This I did, feeling rather mean about it, however, but presently the man returned bringing me a fresh supply of pellets, from which I concluded that he was after all as well pleased with the bargain as I was myself. I had to " pay my footing " with the bow, however, for on trying to use it I only succeeded in smashing the pellets against my knuckles, until I discovered that at the moment of releasing the string the left hand should be pulled sharply to the side, so allowing the bullet to pass, after which I made some fairly good practice.

Min-byin itself proved to be a very trim little village, built on the high bank overlooking the river, and surrounded by a well-built stockade of timber. Without, however, adding to descriptions which I fear may become tedious, two points of interest struck me. In the sand-banks hollows had been scooped out into which the river filtered, so giving the villagers a somewhat purer water supply than the river itself afforded, as these streams are not only the *drinking* places but the *bathing* places also of the wild animals with which these forests teem. The other feature which I noticed was that the women engaged in cutting fuel in the woods wore upon their backs a little basket of wicker-work, which served the purpose of a pocket in which their "kukries"[1] and other impedimenta were carried. I noticed the same custom later in other places, and no doubt this is a common practice throughout the country.

This was my last day with my friends, who were obliged to return to Kokogon. To them I owe a great debt of gratitude for their kindness in organising and "personally conducting" an expedition which was to me one of absorbing interest, and I am not without the hope that at some future time I may again be able to enjoy their genial companionship on such another journey.

The following morning commenced two days of episodes, some of which might have had very unpleasant results, though fortunately all went well in the end.

At dawn a travelling elephant was loaded up with my baggage and commissariat (among which was a live chicken for my dinner), and, accompanied by six servants, I left for Kyet-thoung-doung, where I proposed to spend the night. Among the servants who had gone on ahead were my own boy Chinnasammy, and Moung-Ba, a middle-aged Burman who had been specially attached to me as interpreter, so that when an

---

[1] A heavy sheathed knife used as a chopper.

Through the Forest to Pyinmana

hour later I waved my last adieux to my friends and started on my journey, I was practically alone, my only companion being a small boy who acted as "syce" and guide, and with whom, owing to my ignorance of Burmese, I could not communicate, and my adventures began early.

Behind Min-byin were large paddy fields, across which my path lay, but owing to the pleasant native habit of ploughing up all tracks at sowing-time, the pathway soon vanished into nothingness, and was succeeded by a labyrinth of bunds which led nowhere, and soon caused us to become hopelessly mixed. Time and again we struck what looked like a road leading in the desired direction, but in each case it terminated in impenetrable jungle or doubled on its track.

Presently a native appeared : " Kyet-thoung-doung, eh ?" I queried. Spreading his five fingers and giving a broad sweep of his arm, he indicated about 90 degrees of horizon, so that I was not much the wiser, but knowing that it lay approximately south-east from Min-byin I struck an average, and pushed on through whatever came.

Meanwhile an hour of the cool of the day had been lost, and I was beginning to get irritated, when to my joy I heard the distant groanings of a native cart, and making in the direction of the sounds struck a road, which, however, ran at right angles to my supposed course, and the question then arose as which way to turn. With a bright smile of intelligence, my little guide indicated the left, but after some miles the road, which was generally down-hill and presented every conceivable kind of impediment, took a sharp turn to the north which plainly showed that we had taken the wrong turning and must retrace our steps. Riding down-hill had been bad going, but returning up-hill through tangles of weeds, over fallen timber and slippery mud-slides, was extremely vexatious both to man and beast, and when we reached our starting-point of an hour earlier we were alike tired and cross ; but our direction now proving to be the right one, I settled down more contentedly to recover by steady riding some of the time lost in our wanderings.

I have already referred to the heavy dew hanging on the undergrowth, and on this occasion I was saturated. What particularly annoyed me was the cold dripping of the moisture down my neck and spine, to avoid which I formed the habit of striking any overhanging reeds with my riding switch, so shaking off the dew-drops before meeting the boughs with my head and shoulders. Once in striking aside a bamboo shoot, which would otherwise have brushed across my face, I dislodged a vividly green snake, about two feet in length, which, protected by its colour, lay concealed among the fresh leaves. The snake, which I killed, proved to be a venomous one, and had it struck me would in all probability have put an abrupt termination to my journey ! This bamboo switch, by the way, which I had cut on my first day in the forest, was the only weapon I carried in Burma, and I keep it still as a valued memento of more than one adventure in the country.

A FOREST TAI

Through the Forest to Pyinmana

For the rest of the day my journey was without special feature, the forest being as before grandly beautiful, though perhaps being alone it appeared to me more solemn and impressive than usual. Our road though rough was well defined, crossing hill and dale and through sylvan glades, in which for the first time I saw ferns, though small and of a common variety much like our polypods.

The riding, however, was by no means easy, for these forest roads are terribly bad in many places, being simply deep ruts through sand or laterite, and rough as a water-course. How it is that the native carts do not capsize is to me a mystery, one wheel being often four feet higher than the other, as the patient bullocks drag them over rocks or roots, through ruts and boggy streams with equal indifference! Nothing seems to come amiss to the Burmese driver, who says that wherever a pony can ride a cart can travel! Indeed, I am not sure that they do not put it the other way, and give the cart precedence for facility of transit.

Kyet-thoung-doung was reached in the early afternoon, the tai being splendidly placed on a high bank overlooking the creek, which we had crossed several times on our way.

Here I had my second adventure of the day. While painting the entrance to the village, my "boy" came to inform me that some lads had caught a large snake by the water, and inquired if I would like to see it? I told him to ask the boys to bring it to me, which they did, carrying it between bamboos. Thinking it was dead I told them to put it down until I had time to look at it, when I discovered that instead of being dead it was very much alive, and commenced to wriggle about the legs of my easel! "Kill it," I shouted, but was informed politely that "Burmans do not kill animals," so with my servant's aid I did so myself. The snake was a very handsome one, coloured in alternate bands of coal black and laburnum yellow, with a finely marked pattern running through its scaling. In length it was just over six feet, and I have since been told that it must have been a banded kraite, a particularly deadly species. Unfortunately the head got badly smashed in the process of killing, which decided me not to take the skin, a decision I greatly regret, as this proved to be the only one of its kind I was to meet with.

After the pleasant evenings spent with my friends nothing could exceed the depressing loneliness of my dinner by the light of a single candle, which only served to emphasise the gloominess of my home and its surroundings. Letters and writing up my notes, however, passed the time till "turning in," and I may here mention the fact, and one creditable to every one concerned, that all my letters (which were forwarded from Rangoon) reached me safely and in order of date, the postal arrangements even in these remote wilds being so well organised.

Like the preceding one the following day was not without its adventures. During the night the sounds of wild animals were frequent, and possibly owing to their presence my elephant had wandered far, and, having lost his kalouk, could not be found by his oozi. However, I decided to start for Lewe, where I was to lunch, leaving the servants to load up and follow when the elephant was caught. Accompanied by my little Burman boy I started early as usual, and crossing the creek plunged into a long stretch of jungle, from which during the previous night the roaring of "bad animals" (as my boy put it) had emanated. After a short time my pony began to fidget, and I became conscious of the fact that I was being followed, stealthily but unmistakably, by some beast which the long grasses hid from view. As I was unarmed, the position was distinctly unpleasant, while the thickness of the growth impeded the pony greatly, and we could only proceed at walking pace. This continued for about half an hour, when, the grass coming to an end, I told my boy to hang on, and giving my pony his head "let him go" through the fairly open forest which succeeded it. Whether the animal was a tiger or a leopard I do not know, but the following night a native went down to the creek to sharpen his "dah" and never returned, though the pugs of a tiger on the sand showed what had been his fate, and possibly decided the identity of my "follower" of the previous morning.

This beginning not unnaturally got on our nerves, the pony being perhaps the most upset, and for the rest of the day he was in a state of fidget and excitement. Soon we entered a portion of the forest, deeper, darker, and more solemn than anything I have described.

Burma

Down dark valleys whose end was blackness, or climbing hill-sides where the glinting sunlight penetrated in
patches which intensified the surrounding gloom, it was
an eerie ride, rendered more so by the abnormal silence
which pervaded it. The air was cold, damp, and heavy,
and not a leaf stirred on the shrubs which hid the base
of trees whose lofty trunks vanished into a dark vault
of foliage. "The valley of the shadow of death," was
my mental comment, and my pony's ears lying flat on his
outstretched neck, together with his furtive glances and
little snorts of fear, showed that I was not alone in feeling the awe of the place; even the boy, always light-
hearted and smiling, looked subdued and frightened.

Then an absurdity happened. Wrapped in this
sense of loneliness and oppression, we were slowly
making our way down a long aisle closely hemmed in
by trees, when suddenly, close by my elbow, a shrill
cry broke the silence and the spell which seemed to
bind us. I had just time to notice that it was only a
squirrel scolding at our intrusion as my pony bolted
for the forest, and, crashing and plunging over and
through everything, jamming me up against tree-
trunks or half-strangling me in thorny creepers, placed
my limbs if not my life in greater jeopardy than they
had ever been before or since!

This excitement served to shake off our lethargy,
and the rest of the journey being fairly easy going, we
reached Lewe at mid-day, tired and ready for tiffin.

The dâk here is a Government one and very comfortably furnished, and the kansammah in charge came

IN FOREST DEPTHS

to "salaam," at the same time pouring out a volume of Hindustani of which neither I nor my syce could understand a word. The man appeared to think me very stupid, as indeed I felt, and repeated his statement several times and evidently in different ways, in a vain attempt to reach my understanding. Finally he gave it up and retired to his own quarters, with a grunt of disapproval.

The position was very ridiculous. I wanted my bath, likewise my tiffin, but as we had no common means of communication, I was compelled to possess my soul in patience pending the arrival of my servants and baggage. Hot and tired, how I longed for a whisky-and-soda, and as the hours passed hunger gnawed at me also, and it was not until 4 P.M., ten hours after my chota hazri, that my belated caravan arrived bringing the comforts I was now almost past enjoying. The delay, it appeared, had been caused by the difficulty of capturing the strayed elephant, but this experience taught me never again to go in advance of my commissariat department.

I had still ten miles to ride to Pyinmana, the road being an excellent one from this point, wide, properly metalled, and shaded by trees, and after a very pleasant ride in the cool of the evening, I shortly after dark reached the ever-hospitable bungalow of the Bombay-Burma Trading Corporation.

So ended my ride of over 120 miles from the Irrawaddy to the valley of the Sittang, through scenes which I have no hesitation in describing as the most beautiful I had ever seen, and the recollection of which will always remain with me as a fascinating dream. One or two regrets there are, however, connected with it. I cannot help feeling how enormously the pleasure and interest of the journey would have been enhanced had I possessed even a moderate knowledge of botany or forestry, whose puzzling problems and beautiful growths perpetually tantalised me in my ignorance. Again, should I ever have the good fortune to revisit these forests, a collector's gun and entomological outfit will form important items in my equipment. The large game I do not so much regret,—this is a sport incompatible with the work I had to do, though any "shikarri" would find ample recompense here. But my greatest regret of all is that circumstances so often prohibited my securing sketches of spots of superlative beauty, but which in many cases would have involved a longer halt than was possible, even if conditions of climate and situation made such a course advisable. As it is, I must put these regrets aside, and be thankful to have even *seen* the beauties I have so inadequately described.

Of Pyinmana I can say little, my stay there having been of too short duration to enable me to speak with any conviction, and unfortunately the only sketches I was able to make suffered accidents which have made their reproduction impossible without repainting. It is a pretty spot, however, the views from the bungalow and the little club being charming, and its pagodas and bazaars have many features of special interest.

Through the Forest to Pyinmana

It was always my hope to revisit Pyinmana and renew acquaintance with the friends I made there, as well as record some at least of its most characteristic scenes, but this, like many other of my plans, pressure of time compelled me to abandon.

CHAPTER VII

IN response to urgent invitations, I returned to Rangoon for Christmas week, always a period of social activity, and one in which every one seems to outvie the other in hospitality.

On Christmas Day, for instance, I breakfasted with one friend, lunched with another, spent the afternoon at a garden party, and after a brief visit to the Gymkhana Club, went to a dinner party at 8 o'clock. After dinner was a performance of pierrots and minstrels at the Assembly Rooms, followed by a supper at the Pegu Club! This perhaps was the busiest day of the week, but all were more or less on the same lines, and a few days sufficed to exhaust me, especially after the simple life and early hours of the jungle. I, therefore, decided to limit my stay in Rangoon, and start up the river immediately.

I can imagine no greater contrast to the rough and ready life of the forest or the exuberance of Rangoon than the quiet comfort of a journey up the

Rangoon to Prome

Irrawaddy in one of the fine steamers of the Irrawaddy Flotilla Company. The fleet is a large one, consisting of mail boats, cargo steamers, and ferries, each having good cabin accommodation, and excellent table and attendance; even the ferry boats, on which one seldom requires to pass more than a night, are good in this respect, while the mail steamers are as comfortable as any on the Nile, one in which I travelled even providing a billiard table for its passengers!

As I have frequently heard it suggested that passengers up the Irrawaddy are obliged to undergo considerable discomfort, and are carried up in something in the nature of a barge, it may be a surprise to many to know that the mail steamers, as a rule, measure about 325 feet in length, with a breadth over sponsons of 76 feet; that their tonnage is between 1200 and 1350, and they carry anything up to 2500 passengers, having a speed of about 14 knots.

As, however, travellers are yet few in Burma, the greater portion of space in these steamers is given up to cargo and deck passengers. The cabins are placed on the upper deck, forward of the engines, and in the extreme bow is a promenade deck, where meals are served, and where you can enjoy both the scenery and the breeze, and I may add that in the captains of the steamers in which I sailed I found not only genial companions but a source of valuable information, which I greatly appreciated.

Almost without exception my Rangoon friends advised me not to make the whole journey by water, but by taking the train to Prome avoid some 300 miles of river and creek, which they assured me was without interest. As it was my desire to see the whole navigable length of the Irrawaddy, I fortunately decided against this advice, and found that the lower river was as interesting as anything higher up, though in a different way.

The branch of the river which connects Rangoon with the Irrawaddy proper is no longer navigable, and steamers, therefore, are obliged to drop down stream some fifteen miles and, by way of the Bassein creek, eventually reach the main river at a point called "the hole in the wall," from which a glimpse of the sea is obtainable.

All this is of course tidal water, and very muddy, and at high water the low-lying land is almost entirely submerged. The scenery is generally quiet, the narrow waterway being fringed with mangrove trees and dwarf wild-dates, whose foliage has a peculiar sickly tint due, no doubt, to the constant saturation to which they are subjected. Every here and there is a hut, or little settlement of bamboo dwellings, built partly on the bank and partly over the water, the homes of fishermen who, half naked, paddle about in dug-out canoes, and whose nets, hung over bamboo frames, are drying in the breeze.

Branching right and left from the river are creeks which intersect the Delta in all directions, cutting up the land into islands of greater or less area, between which communication is quite impossible except by means of boats. Some of these islands are under cultivation, but the greater part are covered with jungle and abound in game of all kinds, including tigers. Indeed, I am told that in some places tigers are so numerous as to render landing dangerous.

On what may be called the mainland, however, are enormous tracts of land under rice cultivation, and I believe that these districts produce a large proportion of the total paddy crop of Burma.

Our first stopping-place was Dedaye, a village of amphibious habits, nestling in tropical foliage, amongst which I noticed for the first time the slender stems and graceful crest of the betel-palm.

On the banks were a number of boats, building or undergoing repairs, and waiting for the next monsoon floods to float them off. All these boats were of the typical Burman build, with high sterns and up-tilted bows, and with nicely flowing lines throughout. Even the little dug-out is pretty, both stern and forefoot rising clear of the water in a slight curve which gives an element of beauty to what would otherwise be simply a straight log.

Afloat, these boats, deeply laden with paddy for the Rangoon mills, are extremely graceful, and as their crews of perhaps fourteen or sixteen rowers bend their backs to the long sweeps they use, they unconsciously bring to mind the galleys of ancient Rome, and impress as much by their dignity as by the beauty of their sweeping lines.

In marked contrast are the Chinese boats, which are

utilitarian to the exclusion of all other considerations, while others, equally uninteresting, are manned by Indian coolies, who, with spoon-shaped oars, paddle in an inefficient and hesitating manner most irritating to a waterman.

Returning "laung-zats" and "peingaws" having discharged their cargoes, speed upstream before a breeze which cools the air and breaks the river into wavelets. Under sail the rig of these boats is peculiar. The mast is formed of two bamboos, stepped at the gunwale almost amidships, which, inclining inwards, are bound together at the head, while battens of wood lashed across them form a ladder which takes the place of shrouds and ratlines. An enormous yard, also of bamboo, and which bends upwards on each side from the mast, serves to carry four or more square-cut sails of cotton cloth, some of which are embroidered at the edges, and which can be taken in one by one, according to the strength of the breeze. Above are top-sails spread by a multitude of cords stiffened by two upright bamboos lashed to the yard. The whole forms a confusing net-work of ropes and spars, and, though picturesque enough, I do not think I have ever seen any vessels rigged in a more unpractical manner.

The fact is that the Burmans are no sailors, and their beautiful boats are better adapted for drifting or rowing than for sailing. The sails, which are badly cut and trimmed, can only be used before the wind, and are of no use at all for reaching or beating to windward. The Chinese and other boats almost invariably carry a square sail set as a lug, which, though non-pictorial, being dyed red with cutch, supplies a valuable note of colour among so much greenery.

Ascending the river the land gradually becomes firmer and the banks higher, though still but little raised above high-water mark. Not so completely saturated as the swamp land lower down, the growth on the banks gradually undergoes a change, the mangrove giving place to the tamarind and banyan, while near the villages, such as Maubin, the cool green of the banana groves mingles pleasantly with the more robust foliage of forest trees.

This district is naturally much infested with mosquitoes, which at Maubin I am told exist in such numbers that even the ponies in their stables have to be protected by " meat cages " ! Recently, however, the jungle on the opposite side of the river has been cut down and fired, resulting in a very considerable diminution of the plague. Our steamer moored here for the night, and though the deck and cabin lights attracted enormous numbers of moths and flying insects of all kinds, I do not remember that mosquitoes were particularly numerous, and certainly they caused me little or no inconvenience.

I see from my notes that we left Maubin at 6 A.M. on New Year's morning ; it was beautifully bright but cold, and a soft purple haze hung upon the horizon, through which sunlit trees and gilded pagodas shone. The limpid water reflecting the clear blue overhead acquired that curious colour termed " eau-de-nil," and which one associates peculiarly with Egypt. As the day advanced the heat of the sun made itself felt, and the glare on the water seemed to justify the smoked glasses which the captain and most of the passengers affected. By 10.30 we had reached Yandoon, which is the Irrawaddy end of the creek, which lower down is termed the "Rangoon river." This is a prosperous market town, a very large number of native boats lying up against the river bank, while the smell of "ngapi," [1] which is made here, filled the air. In strolling round the village I was escorted by all the gamins from the streets, who displayed a good-humoured and at the same time well-behaved interest in my, to them, eccentric curiosity with regard to domestic incident.

The village was a good type of a flourishing Burmese centre ; the people, on the whole, seemed prosperous, and the houses were generally well built, and as, in addition to their trade in paddy, Yandoon is one of the few places in Burma where ngapi is manufactured (an article in universal consumption), I have no doubt the villagers are extremely well-to-do. In some respects, moreover, they are quite up to date, many articles exposed for sale in the shops being of the latest European pattern, while in one hut I noticed a middle-aged woman, a huge cigar stuck perkily in the corner of her mouth, busy pedalling away at a sewing machine stitching up a lungyi.

Time did not permit of my making any sketches of Yandoon, as the steamer's stay here was of a very short

---

[1] Partially cured and salted fish.

duration, and indeed, though there are a good many cocoanut-palms and mimosa-trees scattered through its streets, it is not so intrinsically pictorial as many other villages I have visited.

Behind the town were immense tracts of paddy land, and every here and there was a raised platform for the use of men and boys engaged in the scaring of birds in harvest time. I was sorry to notice one fact which became increasingly apparent as we proceeded upstream, which was the substitution of galvanised iron roofing for the more picturesque "thekke," and the use of kerosene tins in place of the beautiful water chatties of native manufacture.

On rejoining the steamer all the small fry of the village who had been my companions on my tour of investigation assembled on the bank to give me a parting salute, some running down the steep incline and plunging into the water, in which they disport themselves like fish.

To me the main interest in Yandoon was centred in the native craft moored along its banks, whose quaint beauty seems to increase the more one sees of them, their extraordinarily high sterns becoming quite a fascination. Many of these structures, already rich with carving, are still further ornamented by projecting sticks on which are stuck inverted soda-water bottles, which glitter in the sunshine. I am told that the rowers frequently have beside them piles of bottles to be used as weapons in case of dacoity, a not unusual occurrence; and as the use of firearms is forbidden to the natives, these bottles serve as a very effective means of defence.

The river here is wide, the banks on either side being low and, generally speaking, heavily clothed with foliage. The scenery is simple in character, consisting generally of a succession of pretty "bits" of con-siderable pictorial value. Here, for instance, crowning a bank of peculiarly soft colouring and texture, is an enormous banyan-tree shading a number of thatched buildings, from amongst which rises a "tagundaing" with its streamer, which marks a shrine. A short distance from it a lofty toddy-palm rises from a mulberry plantation, while close down to the water's edge are a couple of "laung-zats," undergoing repairs at the builders' hands. A simple enough scene, but one in which the beautifully contrasting foliage and local colour, perfectly repeated in the water below, combine to form a picture of great beauty. Indeed, some of these water-side bits are extremely pretty, the different builds and rigs of the boats, the great variety of tropical foliage, and the occasional pagodas or monasteries giving to each its distinctive character; and in all cases additional beauty is derived from the reflection in the water, which, due to its opacity, almost perfectly repeats the life it carries and the picturesque banks which confine it.

During the day Donabyu was reached, the scene of the fight with Bandoola in the first Burmese war, but now largely given up to the manufacture of cheroots, which has become an industry here. In fact, of all

Rangoon to Prome

Burman cheroots those from Donabyu are considered the best and command the highest prices. They are made and the trade entirely conducted by women, but unfortunately it is difficult to ensure the same quality for any length of time from any given maker, for no sooner does the lady proprietress of a cigar manufactory gather a good *clientèle* about her than she either lowers the quality of her cigars, or sells the business as a going concern to some one else, and starts again in opposition !

Henzada was reached after nightfall, the last two hours of our journey being accomplished by means of the electric search-light. The effect of this was very curious when turned upon the banks, the trees appearing to be quite flat, like the wings in a theatre, throwing crisp black shadows upon those beyond in strong contrast with the glowing silver of the illuminated portions. In the band of light which traversed the darkness between the steamer and the shore swarmed thousands of insects, and, as corners in the river were rounded, or the light thrown upon the bank whereon a village stood, all the youngsters of the place would rush pell-mell down the banks to gambol in its weird illumination.

The following morning, having passed the last of the creeks through which the Irrawaddy finds the sea, we entered the undivided water which, coming from an unknown source, is navigable for large steamers for 1000 miles of its length. In many respects the river is like the Nile—its banks are the same high mud walls, cut into terraces by the scour of the water, and crowned with foliage and native villages, and in its flow it has the same oily swirl we know so well in Egypt. The colouring of sky and water is also much the same, the chief points of difference being in the build of the boats and the nature of the vegetation on its banks. On the other hand, the shores of the lower Irrawaddy are not so full of incident as in the case of the Nile. The people do not throng the watering-places as in Egypt, and the absence of cattle on its banks is noticeable. I was rather struck, however, near Myanaung to notice an implement for water-raising almost identical with the "shadoof" of Egypt. This consists of long bamboo arms, erected on a high staging, working on a swivel, and from which depend buckets and ropes with which the water is raised for the cultivation of betel in the farms behind, the raised water being emptied into troughs of split bamboo, which serve as conduit pipes. These are called, I believe, in Burmese "moung-le."

Myanaung is a pretty village, having a village green and a very handsome group of pagodas, which by the way are kept in excellent repair. Close by this principal group, however, is a ruined pagoda, so entirely encircled by ficus that it is difficult to discover that it is not simply a huge tree, and it is only in the dry season when the leaves have fallen that any signs of the masonry of the pagoda are visible.

I found here that there was an English school-master, and many of the native children are learning to speak English, and, unfortunately, to adopt our clothing. I met some boys idling on the green, and asked them why they were not playing football or some other game. Their reply was, " Oh ! this is a holiday." I could not help speculating as to the future of these little prigs ; superior to their parents in education, will they grow up as Burmans, or develop into those swaggering nondescripts now, alas, so often met with in the larger towns in Burma ?

So far the river had been tidal, and the scenery quietly tropical in character. After the second day, however, the aspect of the river changes somewhat, and from the west bank rise hills of gradually increasing height, the beginning of the Arracan Yomas.

Some little distance above Myanaung occurs an interesting feature in Gaudama Hill. This is a cliff which rises from the water's edge to a height of perhaps 150 feet, the whole surface of which is carved into niches containing reclining or seated Buddhas, while many other panels depict incidents of his life. Many of these are gilt, others whitewashed, but the whole effect of the cliff, partially screened as it is by feathery tree-tops and hanging creepers, is striking and curious. Unfortunately the steamers do not stop here, and tourists have no opportunity of a nearer inspection, and as we were under way even a "snap shot" in passing was out of the question, the cliff facing north and the light being insufficient for the purpose. I understand that only at one hour of the day can this be done, and that is when the first flush of sunrise illuminates the cliff, which shortly afterwards, and for the rest of the day, becomes entirely shaded. The hills here as elsewhere in Burma are heavily clothed with vegetation, amongst which the delicate green of the bamboo is always conspicuous. Along the water's edge native life is gradually becoming more apparent, the villages more frequent and more populous, while large herds of cattle wander along the shore. In the fields agricultural pursuits are in full swing, and an ingenious cradle formed of nets on a bamboo frame occupies the fishermen at the water's edge.

This fishing cradle merits description. Two frames of bamboo are fixed at right angles to each other, and swing on a pivot formed by a dug-out canoe. The frame towards the river supports the net, which by means of a rope attached to the other is lowered into the water, where it is allowed to remain for some time. It is presently hauled up, particularly immediately after the passing of a steamer, which frightens the fish in-shore. As the cage is slowly raised, such fish as the net has enclosed tumble into the canoe, while the water pours through the meshes. I asked a Burman one day how it was that a man of his religion could bring himself to kill fish in such a wholesale manner. His reply was ingenuous. "I do not kill the fish," he said ; "if they are stupid enough to get into my net and tumble into my canoe I cannot help it ; besides," he added, "I do not kill them, they die of themselves."

I understand that a license is required for fishing by means of cradle, but a great deal of other fishing goes on

UPSTREAM WITH THE WIND

Rangoon to Prome

in the Irrawaddy and other Burman streams, alike by means of hand-net, spear, and basket. The Burmans are very fond of flesh food, from which their religion practically precludes them ; fish, therefore, is always in great demand, their consciences being clear on the point. In addition to the cradles along the shore, almost every sand-bank in the river is occupied by fishermen, many of whom build huts upon them and reside there the whole of the period between floods. Some of these fishing settlements are in reality villages, to which the fishermen transfer their families and live stock for the season, and in one instance I saw that they had even gone the length of erecting a small pagoda. At Prome quite an extensive and well-built bazaar for the sale of ngapi is erected along the water's edge, which, together with the settlements on the sandbanks, is swept away by the monsoon floods, only to be re-erected the following season as the river falls.

As is the case in all warm-water streams the fish caught in the Irrawaddy are usually coarse and somewhat "flabby," the one great exception being the hilsa, which is usually caught in these tidal waters and is very delicious, quite the best fish to be found in Burma. It is, however, such a mass of bones, all jumbled together like a tangle of fish hooks, that it is almost impossible to separate the meat from the skeleton. I signally failed in my efforts to do so. The native servants, however, have acquired the knack of carving the fish both quickly and neatly.

The whole river trip from Rangoon to Prome is

one of quiet fascination difficult to describe, for though it is without any specially marked feature, every hour brings some object of interest, some fresh incident of native life, or some new feature of the river itself or the varied craft it carries.

Failing other attractions, the deck passengers on the steamer are an endless source of amusement, and the handling of the cargo at the various stopping-places is interesting, and throws considerable light upon the requirements of the people and the nature of the trade carried on.

Here are some items of the cargo carried by the *Beloo*, in which I was travelling :—

Large cases of Japanese safety matches.	Soap, acids, and hardware.
	Sugar.
Oil from U.S.A.[1]	Cocoanut-oil and ngapi.
Dried meat (in bales).	Crockery and lamps (English).
Pickled eggs from China (in sealed air-tight pots).	Cases of "Scotch" whisky (labelled "made in Germany ").
Dried fish from the Straits Settlements.	Flour for native troops (Atta).

These items were gathered at haphazard, and in no way complete the range of a very varied cargo. I was forced to the conclusion, however, from what I saw, that many articles imported into Burma ought to have been of *English* manufacture, instead of coming from other countries—Germany perhaps being our keenest competitor.

[1] The great bulk of the oil carried up-country is refined Burma oil from Rangoon refineries, though a considerable quantity still comes from America.

Rangoon to Prome

Most of the stopping-places on the river are marked by a covered barge moored alongside the bank as a combined landing-stage and warehouse.

As the stage is neared, the crew, who are, I think, mostly Chittagonians, dive into the water, carrying with them a line with which to haul in the hawser. There always appeared to be a good-natured rivalry among them as to who should land first, and as they are all good swimmers these periodical races were interesting to watch.

In a great many places where there is no stage the bow of the steamer is simply run into the bank, and a plank put out from the sponson, up and down which surge the crowds waiting to land or embark, laden with their sometimes bulky impedimenta. Collisions of course ensue, and many a wetting results, in one case the postman carrying H.M. mails being swept off his feet into the river below. He was quickly picked up, however, fortunately without damage to himself or the mail-bags.

Wherever I happened to land I found the people polite and unobtrusive, and even when painting in their villages I was entirely free from any annoyance. The villagers would squat behind me in a semicircle talking in whispers, no noise or rudeness ever occurring, though one young lady to whom I passed my sketch for her inspection, after looking at it for a long time *upside down*, returned it to me with the remark that "she thought it very bad"! As a set-off to this unconscious rebuff was the action of an older woman, who, after shikohing to me herself, made her one-year-old infant place its little hands together and do the same ! It was very pretty, but such graceful acts were not infrequent.

Having promised myself some work at Prome I left the steamer here with much regret. Though one of the older mail boats, I had found the *Beloo* a very comfortable ship in which to travel, while Captain Wright, her commander, seemed unable to do enough to add to my pleasure or further my work. I was very sorry to part company with him, and am glad of this opportunity of acknowledging his many acts of kindness.

WAITING FOR THE STEAMER—EARLY MORNING;

CHAPTER VIII

ONE THOUSAND MILES UP THE IRRAWADDY
(PROME TO BHAMO)

INSTEAD of at this stage entering upon any narration of my experiences at Prome, it will be more convenient, I think, if I conclude my description of the river first, leaving the consideration of this and other towns to a later chapter. On the 11th of January, therefore, I joined the express steamer *India*, and proceeded on my journey towards Bhamo.

Prome seems to me to be the point which naturally determines the upper and lower portions of the river. The tidal waters and flat land of the Delta are past, and from this point upwards the characteristics of the river are entirely those common to all great streams which are subject to periodic floods.

The highlands, which began some little distance south of Prome, continue without interruption so far as the west bank of the river is concerned, the east, or left bank, being still composed of the same high and verdure-clad walls of mud, on whose terraced surface the varying levels of the water are recorded.

Burma

Between these banks the river sweeps in majestic curves, which impress with an ever-growing feeling of bigness and dignity. Some of the reaches are wide, having almost the appearance of an inland sea ; in others the rocky banks confine the stream more narrowly, but in either case it is always impressively beautiful.

In flood time the whole width of the river is open to navigation, but as the level falls this becomes increasingly difficult, a fact plainly demonstrated by the wrecks of steamers and other craft to be met with from time to time.

Like all flood rivers the Irrawaddy changes its course annually, and is at considerable trouble and expense re-surveyed each year by the Flotilla Company as the water falls and the sand-banks begin to appear.

The often tortuous channels are marked by buoys of bamboo, which are anchored by sand-bags, and are differentially coloured according to the side of the channel upon which they are placed. Owing to the glare of sunlight upon the water it was often a difficult matter to pick up these buoys, until one of the captains of the mail steamers suggested the ingenious plan of suspending from the head of the buoy a disc of tin, which, swinging about as the bamboo bent and vibrated in the eddies, caught the sun's rays and flashed its danger signal like a heliograph.

In addition to these precautions, the lead is kept constantly going from either side, while in some of the more difficult passages a pilot launch is stationed in order to give the larger steamers a " lead " through the reach to which it is appointed.

Drift logs, débris of all kinds, as well as an occasional wreck, may at any moment impede navigation, to guard against which the Company have a small fleet of salvage steamers constantly employed in removing obstructions ; and, in order to lessen any risk of grounding, barges are lashed alongside the steamers for cargo purposes during the dry season, thereby reducing their draught to about four feet.

On the Mandalay-Bhamo section these barges are double-decked, and give an added interest to the journey, the main deck being allotted to general cargo and any animals which may be carried, while the upper deck is a native bazaar. The different sections, or stalls, are held by the same people year after year, who, starting from Mandalay well stocked with imports, do a thriving business at all the stopping-places as well as among their fellow-passengers *en route*. On the return journey native produce takes the place of the imported article, and as few of the villages along the river have bazaars of their own, this floating market is the only one available, and the business done is very lucrative. There is great competition among the natives for accommodation on these boats, but so long as they pay their tolls and behave themselves, no holders of stalls are disturbed in their possession, which I am told often pass from one generation to another.

Independent of the regular stopping - places the native frequently manages to board the steamer in a variety of ways. Sometimes in response to their cries the steamer will slow down and the would-be passenger, plunging into the water, is soon alongside and is hauled on board by many willing hands. More generally a dug-out canoe shoots out from the bank, and the boatmen hanging on to the after part of the steamer manage to transfer its passengers and baggage while the steamer is under way. Here is another filled with bright-coloured fruit and vegetables. A half-naked Burman is paddling at the stern, and at the bow squats a woman dressed for the bazaar, and shaded by the usual semi-transparent native umbrella which bathes her in a golden half-tone. Courtesy demands a halt in order to embark so attractive a passenger ; but more imperative was the method adopted in another case, where the canoe, manned by two men with poles, was held up across stream and right in the middle of the only passage available for the steamer, which was perforce obliged to stop. The passenger scrambled in over the bows, caring little apparently for the rating he received from the captain for " stopping the mail."

Of the many incidents of the river none perhaps is more interesting than the studies of human nature frequenting the landing-places and river front. At every stage is the usual crowd of natives landing or joining the steamer, coolies handling the cargo which is brought down seemingly impossible declivities by bullock gharries, to which nothing in the shape of bad roads seems impossible. At various points the shore is stacked high with eng wood,—fuel for the steamer, which is put on board by lusty young women who work by piece work, and do not spare themselves.

Along the river's brink are seated groups of fishermen, offering for barter or for pice the fish their baskets hold, and which from time to time are dipped into the water in order to preserve in them some semblance of freshness ; while against any convenient stone, or baulk of wood, the village " dobie " beats the life and texture out of such garments as he may be engaged in washing. Girls come and go to fill their water chatties or bathe in the river. They are always attractive, and swim like fish in spite of their clinging lungyi, for they always enter the water clothed. There is usually a dry garment in reserve, however, and I noticed that it is held out to the wind and inflated, and then quickly slipped over the body as the wet one falls. Always modest, the Burmese woman is never more so than when bathing. Yet they are by no means bashful or self-conscious, and I was much amused one day in watching the *al fresco* toilet of one of these dusky beauties. The lady in question, carrying a chattie, came down to the water's edge, and, squatting on a small bamboo raft which happened to be there, filled the chattie with water and commenced to wash her hair. Her hair was very long, and she gave it a thoroughly good washing, taking out the tangles from time to time with a small wooden comb ; then quickly twisting it into a knot at the front of her head, she left it to dry in the sun, and drawing out of the chattie a long tail of *false* hair, proceeded to wash it as thoroughly as she had done her own. Stepping into the water, clothes washing followed complete body ablutions, and after slipping on a dry lungyi she gathered up her wet belongings, climbed the bank and disappeared. I have since learnt that this false tail of hair is really the girl's own "combings," which she keeps and makes into an extra coil to add to her already luxuriant tresses on festival days

At Thayetmyo I witnessed a somewhat similar operation. A number of men belonging to a Punjaubi regiment were seated in a line in front of their barracks, each with a bucket of water by his side, and each employed in washing and dressing the long hair of the man in front of him. I do not know how the last man in the line fared, but no doubt his turn came later !

These are some of the incidents of the banks. In midstream the enormous teak rafts drift slowly on their tedious voyage to the sea, others made of bamboo are carrying the heavy pyingado logs which, unable to float, are slung beneath the raft. Each has its crew of almost nude Burmans or Shans, whose duty consists entirely in keeping the head of the raft straight, which they do by means of a number of oars, built of bamboo, which are lashed at either end. Most of their time is spent in drowsing, however, probably the effect of smoking "gungah," [1] and the rafts, swinging across stream, often impede the steamer's traffic, for they are heavy weights to bump into and must be avoided. Many of them are so crowded with huts as to resemble a village afloat, and often carry live stock, while a great many smaller

---

[1] A preparation of hemp seed similar to the *hashish* of Egypt.

rafts have been constructed specially for the transport of cattle, in which a large trade is carried on, and for which the boats or steamers at present on the river apparently do not sufficiently cater.

It would be wearisome were I to dwell at length upon every feature of the river, though a description of a few of its specially characteristic reaches will serve to give a broad impression of the whole.

We left Thayetmyo in the early morning, as soon as the sun had finally dissipated the usual fog, the river being wide and its scenery of the same quiet character I have already described.

Under a hot sun and almost cloudless sky the oily stream reflected each object, and against its deep-toned blue the red sails of the boats and glittering sand-banks stood out powerfully.

To the west the blue height of Mount Victoria is only hazily visible above the wooded Yomas, while on the east the interesting but now extinct volcano Popa dominates the arid plain which surrounds it. On the river bank and standing out in bold relief against the distant mountains is Pagan-ngé, or little Pagan, its gilded and white pagodas glimmering among the foliage.

On the opposite side of the river a gentle slope, covered with trees, among which appear the low-pitched roofs of native houses, leads to a succession of zayats and kyaungs which climax in an abruptly conical hill, also crowned by its pagoda.

At intervals along the banks are little patches of cultivation, onions, peas, and beans being planted in the soft mud as the water recedes. In the shallows wild geese or cranes are fishing, or basking by hundreds on the banks, and cormorants rest idly on the surface of the river or fly, startled, across the steamer's bows. Being January, autumn tints are beginning, and here and there on the hillsides the white smoke of forest fires adds to the general sense of warmth and dreaminess. Indeed, not even on the Nile can one so thoroughly enjoy an idle rest, or one wherein the scenery so fully accords with one's dreamy instinct, as on these quiet reaches of the Irrawaddy. Here all nature is serenely beautiful, and from a distant village the rich softness of a hpungyi's gong stealing over the limpid water seems to strike the mellow keynote of the scene.

In its general character the scenery of the Irrawaddy is one of sun-bathed beauty, placid and perhaps a little commonplace looked at broadly, for these beautiful serrated hills, which rise tier upon tier to mountains of considerable height, are so completely swathed in tropical vegetation, that outlines which might under other circumstances be full of character are so smoothed down by vegetable growth as almost to appear like mossy mounds, which the passenger enjoys with contentment though without stimulation; yet every bit of this river scenery is full of interesting points, which excite inquiry or demand a mental note. It is startling, for instance, to pass in one week from the dark-green mangrove swamps of the Delta to the dry zone, where many of the trees are already bare and the rest in their

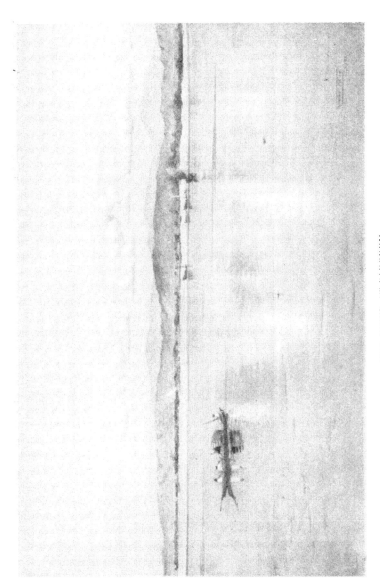

THE RIVER AT PAKOKKU

autumn foliage. The coloration is splendid, ranging from the pale green of the bamboo to the scarlet-coated cotton-tree, or the more lovely terra-cotta tint of the dhak. Most of the tree-trunks are sun-bleached and white, the general effect of the colour scheme being a mauve or pinkish tint, relieved at the water's edge by the vivid green of trees and shrubs, whose supply of moisture is perennial.

On my return journey some months later, after the dry season and forest fires had denuded the trees of their foliage, the character of the river scenery had undergone a marked change, and what on the upward journey had appeared as gently rounded hillocks now revealed themselves as bold and rugged mountains, full of distinction and in strange contrast to their gentler aspect of spring.

If the first dominant characteristic of the river scenery is the luxuriance of its forest growth, the second surely is the enormous number of pagodas which adorn both banks of the river throughout its entire length. It would almost seem as though the Burman regarded each hillock as specially provided by nature as a pediment for his religious buildings. Their number is surprising and may, I think, be reasonably taken as a proof of the activity of the Buddhist religion. Most of them, however, are ruinous, for though the builder of a pagoda obtains "merit" by so doing, no reward falls to the lot of the *repairer* of such edifices, consequently any one able to do so prefers to build a pagoda of his own rather than, by repairing or beautifying an existing shrine, add to the kudos attaching to its founder. This belief explains the multiplication of pagodas, though it does not apply to some of the more noted shrines, such as the Arracan pagoda at Amarapura, the Shwe Dagon in Rangoon, and several others in the country which are the objects of pilgrimage, and upon which devotees lavish gold freely.

It is curious to notice the extraordinary positions in which some of these pagodas are placed : in the heart of the forest and unfrequented jungle they are constantly met with ; on the crest of a precipitous rock in the middle defile is a beautiful little zedi which must have been erected under conditions of extreme difficulty ; but most extraordinary of all, perhaps, is that one built on the top of a boulder balanced on the edge of a precipice at Kyiak-Ti-Yo in the Thaton district.

There are two spots on the river which, beyond any others, emphasise this extraordinary predilection of the Burmese for pagoda-building,—the one, that beautiful succession of terraced hills, literally covered with pagodas, all that now remain of the old capital Sagaing ; the other, that magnificent congregation of temples, dating from the eleventh century, which render the now ruined and deserted city of Pagan unique in Burma.

I will never forget my first approach to Pagan in the early morning. The river wound along the base of fair-sized hills which, rather curiously, were almost entirely barren, though glorious in colour as the early morning sun illuminated them. The opposite side consisted of the abrupt edge of the plain, which rose gradually to the base of Mount Popa, still visible in the distance. Along the edge of this muddy cliff and stretching far inland were the ruined monuments of Pagan, mostly square-built temples surmounted by cupolas and pinnacles, different in character from anything I had hitherto seen, though the bell-shaped form occurs in the golden Shwe Zigon and in the little Bu pagoda which rises in a succession of terraces from the water's edge.

Unfortunately the steamers do not stop at Pagan itself, though many picturesque and striking views of the old city are obtainable as the river winds in sweeping curves round the enormous sand-banks to the north, until twenty minutes later the steamer enters the expansive reach which lies above the city, and draws up at the landing-place of Nyaung-u, the modern successor to the glorious old city five miles away. It is somewhat unfortunate that tourists have not the opportunity of thoroughly exploring old Pagan, not only one of the most historically interesting spots in Burma, but one well worth seeing on pictorial grounds alone. As it is, no means of communication exists between Nyaung-u and Pagan proper, and at the best the length of time the steamers remain here is barely sufficient for the most active of her passengers to undertake the tedious walk which will enable him to enjoy a brief half-hour in the beautiful Shwe Zigon pagoda. I would like to suggest the possibility of establishing a rest-house in the old town, under the charge of an English-speaking custodian, where visitors might remain until the arrival of a following steamer, and so be able to see something at least of its more celebrated monuments. Through the courtesy of friends I was enabled to stay for some little time here, but with that I will deal in another chapter.

Between here and Mandalay is an interesting reach of the river where, at Pakokku,[1] the Chindwin empties itself into the Irrawaddy. The banks on either side are flat, but evidently fertile, while the river is probably at its broadest point. To the north, behind the belt of foliage which crowns the banks, lies a plain which terminates in the blue mountains that lie between the Mu river and the Irrawaddy at Sagaing, against which stands out in bold relief the white circular dome of the enormous Kaung-Hmu-Dau pagoda.

This stretch of the river was peculiarly lovely as I saw it. In the soft blue of the sky float delicately tinted clouds, whose reflections long drawn down the glassy surface of the water seem to add to the feeling of fulness and expanse which characterise it. Along the bank slide the always fascinating native boats, while others glide slowly, almost sleepily, along the river. Suddenly the stillness of the scene is broken, as the powerful " marsia," pursuing the small fry on which it

[1] Pakokku, by the way, is the great centre of boat-building on the Irrawaddy. From here also the Flotilla Company run a service of steamers 274 miles up the Chindwin to Kindat, with an extension line of smaller vessels to Homalin, 147 miles farther. I was unable to make this journey myself, but I am told that the scenery on the Chindwin is particularly fine.

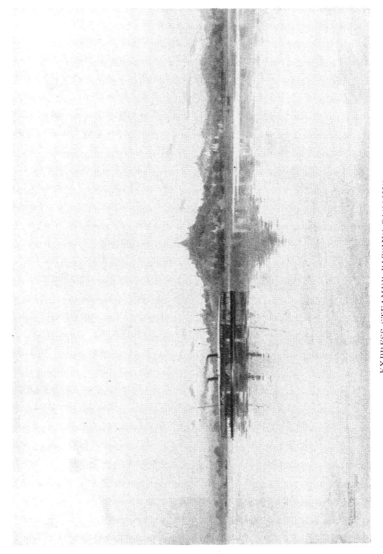

EXPRESS STEAMER PASSING SAGAING

feeds, skims the surface of the water like a silver flash, sometimes leaping clear of the water in its impetuosity, while close by on a sand-bank an alert black and white heron bides his time to strike the surfeited fish. To the south and east the river is full of shoals, on which thousands of water-birds, principally geese, are busy feeding, a sight very tempting to a sportsman ; and as the steamer could not by any possibility approach within range for a shot-gun, we tried a few long-range shots with Martini-Henrys, but without success, for though in one or two cases we saw " feathers fly " we failed to bag a bird ; what became of the ricochetted bullets remained a problem ! I noticed one of these geese swimming in the channel which, after a dive, had managed to catch a large fish by the tail. Then ensued an interesting struggle. Too big to swallow and too heavy to lift, the goose's head was almost continuously under water, and it stood a very good chance of being drowned. However, by vigorous swimming and beating the water with its wings, it managed to tow its unmanageable captive and land it high and dry upon a sand-bank, where, after recovering from the exhaustion of the fight, it devoured it at leisure.

The approach to Mandalay is very pretty, the limpid river flowing between shelving banks of sand surmounted by forest trees, behind which the lofty Shan hills rise hazily into the air. From among the green foliage of the banks appear the white temples of Amarapura, and Mandalay Hill, also crowned by a speck of white, shows up ruddy in the sunlight.

Burma

Presently the fort at Ava comes into sight, its red-brick structure, covered by many pagodas, jutting into the water from its wooded base ; while on the opposite side, from the picturesque landing-place for the railway ferry, commence the beautiful undulations of the Sagaing hills.

This succession of hills forms one of the distinctive notes of the river. The local colour of the rock is rich and varied, the pearly grey of the shingle along the beach contrasting with the ochres and reds of the exposed portions of the rock above, while from among the verdure with which the hills were generally clothed innumerable pagodas, gleaming white, or brightly red where time had removed the outer coating of stucco, rose in successive tiers to the central hill, where the largest of these pagodas crowned the apex. From each of these pagodas flights of steps, bounded by whitened walls, led to the lower levels, and from among the trees which marked the extreme height of the river, enormous leogryphs seemed to repel rather than invite the pilgrim to ascend the approach to the temple they guarded.

The river is narrow here, and swirls in deep and rapid eddies along the shore, across which gaily coloured sampans act as ferries for dainty ladies and their families from Mandalay, bent upon a picnic, or perhaps devotions, at one of the more noted shrines.

Sagaing is an old capital of Burma, and, with Pagan, shares the distinction of occupying a position of dignity.

In marked contrast, Mandalay, which lies some distance from the water, on low-lying ground, is mean in its approach, and, except for the fact that three or four landing-barges are moored along the banks instead of one, has little to differentiate it from the poorest village on the river.

From here a bi-weekly service of steamers runs to Bhamo, but as their dates of sailing may not always be suitable, an alternative route is offered by way of Katha, at which point a daily service of ferry steamers meets the trains, and thirty-six hours later reach what is practically the frontier town, and the limit of organised steamboat traffic on the Irrawaddy.

I travelled both ways—going up *via* Katha and returning all the way by river.

Leaving Mandalay in the early afternoon by train, Amarapura shore was reached at about 4 P.M., when baggage and passengers were transferred to the ferry which was to take us across the river.

During the time so occupied, a very refreshing tea was served, and on reaching the landing-place at Sagaing the train was alongside ready to receive us. Here I found that without any request on my part the stationmaster at Mandalay had wired to have a carriage specially reserved for me, an act of courtesy which I appreciated not only for its own sake, but also because it enabled me to offer to a friend more comfortable quarters for the night (for we slept in the train) than would otherwise have been possible for him to obtain ; this coach, moreover, was marked " through," and so saved us the worry of a change of carriages at Naba junction in the early morning.

Burma

The line runs along the western side of the Sagaing hills, now glowing in the sunset. To the west stretches the great plain of arable land through which the Mu river winds its devious way towards the Irrawaddy. In the far distance, blue against the sunset sky, rise the hills which border on the Chindwin, their bases already lost in the rising mist which shortly afterwards hides everything from view.

In the early morning, as we approached Naba, the sunrise was very beautiful. To the east were mountains, deep purple against the rosy sky, and partially reflected in the irrigation water which covered a foreground of paddy land, broken at intervals by patches of forest growth. From the wet earth rose wreaths of mist, winding slowly and snake-like among the trees and up the sloping valleys, until, at a certain elevation it blew off in clouds. Through these patches of vapour the early sun shone in slanting beams, gilding the cane-brakes and tree-trunks, which glowed in contrast with the pearly greyness of the rest of the landscape. It was a lovely and mysterious effect, quickly succeeded by the full light of day, and our own rapid passage downhill through rich forest scenery until, at 9 A.M., we reached Katha.

Here our steamer, the *Pouktan*, was waiting to embark us, starting upstream half an hour after the arrival of the train.

The scenery above Katha is of the usual richly wooded character, beautiful and varied as ever, but calling for no special comment until at sunset we

IN THE SECOND DEFILE OF THE IRRAWADDY

moored for the night at Shwegu. Close to, on a spit of sand by the water's edge, a native festival was in progress. Here a town of booths had been constructed, properly laid out in streets, and in its centre a pagoda. Many thousands of people thronged its bazaars, enjoying the pwes, nautches, and other amusements common to Burmese festivals. The river was alive with boats, and the blaze of colour furnished by the crowd was quite the most brilliant I had yet seen, and was admirably set off by its background of tree-clad hills.

This festival, which I believe is called the Chundau-pya, is an annual one, and is frequented by people from the whole surrounding district.

The following morning we entered the middle defile, and I was on deck early so as to miss nothing of what is perhaps the strongest and most inspiring piece of scenery on the whole Irrawaddy. As I came on deck in the grey dawn the river was enveloped in fog. Outside everything was dripping, and in our state-rooms even the contents of our portmanteaux were damp and clammy, so penetrating are these morning mists. The banks were hardly visible, though the river is narrow here, and the swiftly flowing water was almost black in the lurid gloom which enshrouded us.

Almost suddenly the mist rose from the water and hung upon the hills in heavy clouds just tipped with sunlight. Below, in deepest shade, appeared the narrow entrance to the defile itself, two walls of purple blackness between which still hung a slowly melting film of grey. It was a very striking effect, perfectly repeated in the absolutely still water. Very weird it was too as our steamer plunged into this narrow gulf, from which apparently there was no exit, until the sun finally dissipated the last of the fog and revealed the whole majesty and beauty of the scenery.

Now only about 200 yards in width, the river is bounded by precipitous hills, which form a narrow winding valley through which the confined water flows in swift but silent eddies.

The whole passage of the defile, which occupies several hours, is one of extreme beauty, culminating at a point where a perpendicular cliff rises 800 feet clear out of the water, at the foot of which, crowning a pinnacle of rock at the water's edge, is the little Let-saung-pan pagoda. From the brink of the river to the crest of the hills is a dense mass of vegetation, every crevice in the rocks affording foothold for forest tree or creeper. Being winter the trees on the higher levels are almost bare, exposing limestone bluffs coloured with streaks and patches of red. Lower down the golden brown of withered bamboo clumps contrast with the vivid green of orchids. Along the water's edge the dark-leaved banyan is still covered, and the white and green blossom of the mango mingles with the flaming scarlet of the cotton-tree or the purple cones of the wisteria. It was all extremely beautiful, especially as the reflections in the water were almost perfect ; and if this scene alone constituted the interest of the Irrawaddy it would amply reward the traveller for his journey.

Prome to Bhamo

Bhamo was reached at 11 A.M., of which little town I will have something to say later.

This point, however, 1030 miles above Rangoon, terminated my river trip, for though the scenery of the upper defile and the river to Myitkyina is extremely beautiful, I am told, no service of steamers is provided on these upper reaches, and the special launch which had kindly been arranged for me, through some accident was not available.

On the downward journey were many points of interest, which I have not yet touched upon. Passing through the defile from the other direction only served to add to the strong impression already received, and gave a second opportunity of noting many features of grandeur or of beauty which at the first passage escaped observation. Judging by the number of fishing cradles along the banks, and the many hundreds of cormorants which I saw, the river here must be peculiarly well stocked with fish, and I noticed many new and beautiful growths along its wooded banks.

At a point lower down the river were numbers of elephants bathing in the stream. These had just been caught in an adjacent "keddah,"[1] and only a week previously were roaming wild in the forests. At Tigyaung is a great and most picturesque bathing ghaut, and some little way below Katha is the lower defile. This cannot be compared with the one I have described, but it is of extreme interest nevertheless, winding and rocky, and is simply a variant in the general beauty of the river.

---

[1] The large corral into which wild elephants are driven and captured.

Burma

Presently Thabeikkyin is reached, where ponies are being laden with packs for the ruby mines, three days' journey inland. Close by is a rocky islet, on which stand a pagoda and monastery, the priests of which are accredited with a curious power over the fish in the river, which respond to their call and are fed by hand.

It was interesting also to notice the changed aspect of the scenery in the hot weather compared with the early spring, when I started upstream. The river had fallen considerably, and the banks stood higher out of the water, thereby changing one's point of view.

The luxuriant foliage of spring had given place to bare trunks and apparently barren hill-sides, now streaked with black—the tracks of forest fires whose smoke was added to an atmosphere already heated and opaque, while at night the hills were illuminated with sinuous paths of flame.

At one place, many miles away from the nearest fire (none indeed being in sight), continuous showers of soot, charred leaves, and twigs fell upon our deck in midstream, and during the period of these forest fires the whole air seemed to become opaque, and even at night was so dense that stars could not be seen below 30° above the horizon.

Many other points of interest occur to me, too numerous to describe fully : the huge pagoda and bell at Mingun, the fort at Minla, and the little frontier station which, in the king's time, marked the boundary between British and Native Burma. Here still stand the two telegraph offices, each beside the pillars which marked the frontier. In those days a telegram from Rangoon to Mandalay would be received by the British postmaster at his office, who, crossing the intervening space would retransmit the telegram through the Burmese office, paying for it as a new message. The Burman in his turn was supposed to do the same, when he had any money, but I am told that messages often used to remain in his hands for days before being sent on !

Though my description of the life and scenery of the river is necessarily very incomplete, perhaps I have said enough to give a broad impression of some of its essential features. Perhaps, not unnaturally, I have compared it to the Nile, with which it has many features in common, and though the local interest varies it is in no way less interesting or beautiful.

Altogether the Irrawaddy trip is one of surpassing interest, and the fine fleet of the Irrawaddy Flotilla Company serves the tourist well. I have travelled by many of their steamers, mail boats, cargo boats, and little ferry steamers, and have in each case found the accommodation, table, and attendance quite beyond reproach, indeed, not even on the Nile is the comfort of passengers more carefully regarded.

CHAPTER IX

TWO CAPITALS

NEVER were preconceived ideas so completely shattered as were my own with regard to Mandalay ! I had expected to find a handsome city of Oriental character, instead of which it proved to be as mean as its river approach.

Climbing the high bund which protects the low-lying city from inundation, a drive of two miles or more, through streets lined with huts as poor as any I had seen in the country, brought me to the " fort," in the immediate neighbourhood of which is the only part of the city which can boast of any architectural pre-tension, though even here hovels lie between "pukha "[1] built shops or the bungalows of residents.

It must be remembered, however, that Mandalay is but fifty years old, and the ancient habit of the Burmans of removing their capitals to new sites as kings or dynasties succeeded each other, has tended to check the building of anything more permanent than a wooden house. Pagodas and religious edifices are, of course, an

[1] "Proper," *i.e.* of masonry or brick.

exception to this rule, and Mandalay, like other large centres in Burma, possesses many of extreme beauty.

The city is well planned, however, and is laid out in rectangles. Four main thoroughfares, called A, B, C, and D Streets, run at right angles to the river ; crossing these are others, which are numbered, though many have names also, such as 29th Fire Station Road, 84th Bazaar Street, etc. etc., a system which, though hardly picturesque, has its advantages, for such an address as "the corner of B and 22nd Streets" could not well be mistaken. Generally the streets are wide and shaded by trees, but are, as a rule, badly paved and very dusty. Each has its public fountain or well, at all times of the day thronged by a continual succession of figure groups, and at frequent intervals, rising from among the foliage which hides much of the poverty of the place, are handsome pagodas, kyaungs, or Chinese temples, which come upon one as a surprise, and please accordingly.

The commercial centre lies at the south-west corner of the fort, and appears to be prosperous, though the stucco buildings are as devoid of character as those of Alexandria or Port Said. For the rest, the town is simply an enlarged Burmese village, dilapidated but picturesque.

But though their environment is somewhat sordid, the people themselves wear the gayest of gay costumes, and appear to be happily unconscious of their surroundings, which, however, they make some attempt to beautify by planting about their homes sunflowers, geranium, hybiscus, poinsettia, and other flowers ; and

THE IRRAWADDY BANKS NEAR MYINGYAN

with some deference to the demands of taste, colour the corrugated-iron roofings of their houses a dull terra-cotta, which robs the material of some of its uncompromising ugliness.[1]

The Chinaman is much in evidence, and, as usual, has a good house and looks prosperous and happy ; the Burmans also look happy, because they allow nothing on earth to worry them. Indian natives are numerous, but by comparison appear mean and cringing, though their women walk with agility and grace, while the native regiments and police compel our admiration.

Broadly, Mandalay differs little from Rangoon so far as its inhabitants are concerned, except in one particular, and that is, that its alien peoples *are* alien, and the Burman predominates. It is a Burmese city built for Burmans, and, excepting for a few of the commercial streets, almost solely occupied by them.

Food-stuffs and fabrics seem to form the bulk of the trade of Mandalay, and the streets are bright with groups of animated ladies seeking fresh adornment in the bazaars, or displaying the latest fashions in figured silks and parasols as they promenade. Sober business is only suggested by the houses of the Indian money-lenders, curiously decorated in red and white, whose evil influence extends far beyond Mandalay to the mortgaged crops of the farm-lands ; while the reckless

[1] The use of corrugated iron is becoming more and more general in Burma. Not only has it entirely supplanted the pretty wood shingles formerly used for roofing, but in many cases entire houses are built of it and sheet-iron, and with extreme ingenuity the builders (who are mostly Chinese) often manage to invest them with some architectural character.

gambler (and Burma is full of them) finds accommodation at one of the many Chinese pawn-shops, whose sign and lantern of vivid red strike a bold note of colour in the streets.

Among the infinite variety of delicate tints which glorify the streets of Mandalay, one costume alone appeared to me to be disagreeable in colour, and that is the "yellow robe of poverty" of the hpungyi. The cloth is coloured by a dye extracted from the cutch wood by boiling, which imparts a vivid and raucous yellow tint to the material treated. In a few instances where old garments, sun-bleached and faded, have been patched by a newer material, a little variety of tint renders the costume somewhat more picturesque, but as a rule the colour is harsh and unpleasant; the lines and folds of the costume, however, are distinctly good, it being worn somewhat after the fashion of the Roman toga, the right arm and shoulder being exposed.

No type is more common in the streets than the hpungyi, who every morning sallies forth to collect "sun," as the offering of food is called. No request for alms is ever made, whatever is given being the voluntary and spontaneous act of the donor. Each monastery, however, has its own particular quarter from which to collect, the work being done by priests and novices, each of whom has a particular number of houses upon which to call. Some with bowls in their hands, others carrying a larger receptacle, slung on a pole resting on the shoulders of two of them, and accompanied by the sound of a gong, they regularly and in silence present themselves at the various thresholds in their district, the food, consisting largely of rice, being equally silently placed in the receptacles without any exchange of compliments or thanks.

The most distinctive feature of Mandalay is perhaps the fort, in and about which are the houses of the principal residents and Government officials, military quarters, and the supremely picturesque palace of the king. Built by Mindon Min, Thebaw's father, the fort is a space of $1\frac{1}{4}$ miles square, surrounded by a high battlemented wall of red brick, in which are twelve gates, each surmounted by a handsome pyathat of carved teak. Each gate is screened by a masonry traverse; and at a distance of 20 yards from the wall, and entirely surrounding the fort, is a moat, 100 feet wide and about 12 in depth, crossing which five bridges give access to the principal gates. The moat, which forms the main supply of drinking-water for the town, is covered with purple lotus and is the haunt of ibis and other waders. The water is much the colour of weak tea, has a strong flavour, and cannot, I think, be wholesome; but, especially in the evening, when picturesque groups of people of varied costume and type assemble to draw their drinking-water, it forms one of the prettiest views in Mandalay.

Beside each gate is a large round post of teak, on which, on an iron plate, is inscribed in Burmese characters the following curious proclamation :—

The extraordinary Gate of the Great Golden Royal City which was founded on the night of the 6th after 3 beats

Burma

(of gong)[1] at 4 Nayi and 2 pads o'clock[2] of the entry of Monday 7th waning Kason 1221.[3]

Such a pronouncement prepares one for the names of the gates themselves, which certainly do not err on the side of modesty! Among these are : " Receiving submission of the whole island." " Melodious drum." " Conspicuous." " Mandalay's head." " Receiving submission of 10,000 nations," etc.

From these gates wide roads run parallel to each face of the wall, and lead to the gardens which surround the palace itself. Thanks to a wealth of varied foliage, all gardens in Burma are pretty, and in this case ornamental waters add greatly to their charm. The palace itself is in reality a collection of twenty or more separate buildings, all built of specially selected teak brightly painted and gilded, and having the same upturned eaves and carved ornamentation common to all royal or religious buildings in Burma. It has many audience-chambers, in each of which is a carved and gilded throne. Above the principal one towers the lofty and elegant pyathat called by the Burmans " the centre of the universe "; on either side is a large hall, one now being used as the English church, the other remaining in its original condition, a large open pavilion supported by rows of columns of teak-wood which, together with the roof, are covered with gold-leaf. Behind are several other buildings, used as domestic offices or lesser chambers of audience, each of which is gilded and contains a throne richly decorated and

[1] 3. A.M.   [2] 1. 48 A.M.   [3] 23rd May 1859.

THE MOAT AT MANDALAY

standing on a raised platform, access to which is obtained from behind by a passage and door which admitted the monarch to his throne.

On the west side is the queen's palace, which contains the largest of these audience-chambers. Here in 1875 the special envoys sent by the Viceroy of India to conclude a treaty with Mindon Min were compelled to remove their boots and, kneeling at the threshold, carry on their negotiations with the king, who, with cool insolence, surveyed them through opera-glasses from his throne at the farther end! By a strange irony of fate this particular portion of the palace is now the Upper Burma Club! Though nominally confined to members, natives constantly wander through it, and it is no uncommon sight to see a group of Burmans calmly inspecting the picture papers on the tables before continuing their stroll through the palace precincts, and I was much amused on one occasion while looking at the papers, to see the doors of the throne suddenly fly open and a lady tourist, clad in helmet and white duck, step on to the dais. She appeared very much surprised to find herself so suddenly introduced to a room full of men, and retired precipitately. The question of our using this building as a club is a source of much discussion. The Burmans, not unnaturally, dislike it, and have made several attempts to fire it, as they have already successfully done with other buildings within the fort ; I cannot but feel, however, that it is better to use it for *any* purpose and so ensure one portion at least of a really interesting pile being kept

Burma

in order, rather than hand it over to the Burmans to be destroyed or allowed to go to wreck and ruin.

Since I painted my picture of the palace front the pyathat has, I hear, collapsed, and no doubt the whole structure would sooner or later follow suit unless carefully watched. To-day, I understand the Club is housed elsewhere, a new church erected outside the fort, and the whole palace carefully preserved as an ancient monument ; its buildings are quite unique, and would form an excellent and appropriate home for a museum of Burmese art.

It would be tedious if I were to describe the whole of the palace at the time of my visit, but parts were extremely interesting. In the Club room is a large screen dividing the reading and dining rooms, effectively panelled in glass mosaic and mirrors, which, though tinselly in a way, has, like the thrones, a certain barbaric splendour; and in a gallery connecting this with other buildings is a massive balustrade of wood, the turned pilasters of which are composed of bottle-green glass. The effect of this in the sunlight, and amid so much vermilion and gold, is very striking and harmonious. Throughout the palace the roofs are entirely of corrugated iron, which, possibly on account of their height and large superficial area, do not offend. In the palace grounds are many other buildings, all of some particular interest, but which have been so fully described in other books that it would be idle on my part to enlarge further on the subject.

One of the great sights of Mandalay is the queen's

golden monastery, an ornate structure of teak elaborately carved and gilded, and certainly as fine an example of native architecture as any in the country. Originally all the wood - work, and the stucco buttresses of the steps leading on to the platform, were covered with vermilion before being gilded, and as successive rains gradually wore off much of both, exposing the warm colour of the wood itself, the combination of tint is simply splendid in its richness of tone, the effect of which is further heightened by the cool glass mosaic and silver inlay which distinguishes the doors.

The surroundings of the monastery, however, are very dirty, and curs yelp and snap at all intruders. The priests I found to be most kind and affable, and through the medium of an interpreter I often enjoyed a chat with them while resting in its cool and equally ornate interior. This is only one of many such buildings, all of which are enriched with carving and pleasantly surrounded by groves of trees, among which are the pilgrims' rest-houses.

Mandalay is as rich in pagodas as in monastic buildings ; many are of great beauty, though none approach the Shwe Dagon in scale or magnificence, and the most beautiful of all, " The Incomparable," has been destroyed by fire, though much of its fine stone carving remains. Of the others perhaps the most interesting is Mindon Min's great shrine, the " Kuthodau." Here the pagoda proper is surrounded by 729 cupolas, each of which contains an alabaster slab upon which is engraved a chapter of the Pali Bible, the whole being surrounded by a wall in which are two highly ornate entrance gates of moulded plaster.

Opposite the Kuthodau is an interesting group of pagodas and zeyats in carved wood or moulded plaster, of widely different designs and detail of ornament, in which Keinnaya[1] and figures of various kinds applied as enrichments of the various moulded courses are a very striking feature. In the centre of the group is an ugly unfinished pile, containing a huge marble figure of Gaudama, 25 feet in height, while behind lies Mandalay hill, around whose base and peeping from out its pretty woods are many others of greater or less architectural interest.

The road round Mandalay hill is very pretty, and is the pleasantest drive in the neighbourhood ; interesting kyaungs and Burmese hamlets lie hid among the trees, which give beauty to the road, and on the west side is the racecourse, where very successful race-meetings are held regularly.

All through the town are pagodas of considerable size, and on the south, at Amarapura, is the celebrated Arracan pagoda, one of the great shrines of Burma, to which constant streams of pilgrims resort from all over the country. This pagoda is built in the form of a square tower, rising in a series of diminishing terraces, each embellished with carved battlements with higher finials at the corners. The whole is gilded and its

[1] "Keinnaya" represents the body of a woman in court dress with the wings and legs of a bird.

"THE CENTRE OF THE UNIVERSE." MANDALAY

effect is very graceful, though it is so completely hemmed in by bazaar buildings, zeyats, etc., that I failed to find any point of view from which to paint it.

On the only occasion on which I visited it, it was thronged with worshippers, so that I was unable to see the brass Buddha, twelve feet in height, which occupies the shrine. It is the custom for pilgrims to dab gold-leaf on to the figure, which, with the exception of the head, is now covered with gold to the depth of several inches.

All about the pagoda precincts, and even among those praying, were stalls displaying curios, food, or toys ; but prettiest of all, and most fragrant in the warm close air, were those for the sale of cut flowers which, however, were hardly more beautiful than the exquisite tints and textures in which the worshippers were clad.

This time of year (February), between reaping and sowing, is a period when all the country people come into the capital to worship at one or other of the most famous shrines, and mixing with the Burmans present were representatives of nearly every race or type to be found in Burma. One Karen girl particularly caught my attention : rosy-cheeked and regular in features, she was quite the prettiest woman I had seen in the country. Almost involuntarily I exclaimed, " Well, you *are* a beauty ! " Blushing rosy red, the maid, though of course ignorant of the words I used, took my evident compliment in good part, and with a pretty little " shikoh " returned her thanks.

Burma

Behind the pagoda were two large sacred tanks, filled with what was at one time water, but which is now literally green slime and alive with turtles. I found the bazaar people calling to them and feeding them with sweetmeats, no doubt an "act of merit," so I also spent a few annas in a basket of rice cakes to do the same. Whether it was that the turtles were overfed, or, which is extremely probable, found it difficult to make their way quickly through the thick and greasy element in which they lived, I do not know, but the hawks, which literally swarmed about the place, nearly always succeeded in picking up the savoury morsel before a turtle could reach it.

Many incidents added to the picturesqueness of the temple enclosure : groups of musicians with their quaint instruments, here a reciter of poetry, or again a soothsayer telling the fortune of a credulous client ; but the heat and the flies and the smell from the tanks put a period to one's enjoyment of even such a brightly picturesque scene as this.

It constantly struck me as curious that a Burmese crowd, always light-hearted and happy, is never more so than when participating in some religious function. No matter how solemn the occasion, the spirit of carnival would seem to dominate all other feelings. I noticed this particularly on the occasion of a " hpungyi-byan," which, with great good fortune, took place during my residence in Mandalay.

A hpungyi-byan, which being interpreted means, "the burning or cremating of a hpungyi," is a ceremony of such rare occurrence that even a senior Government official, who came with me on that occasion, had never before witnessed one.

For a week or more certain quarters of Mandalay had been in a state of quiet ferment in preparation for the event. The aged priest, who had died a year previously, had been a man of some notoriety. He had been " ringed " by Mindon Min, and was looked up to as a cleric of great sanctity and position. So the " venerable " was preserved in sawdust and honey till the time arrived to do him public honour. Hence the compound of his particular pagoda had for a week past been turned into a fair, crowded by jolly, laughing men and women, all thoroughly intent upon enjoying the " show," and without much thought, I am afraid, for the departed religionist, or paying much attention to the lesson his life was supposed to teach.

The square in which the pagoda stood was practically full of booths and large pagoda-like structures of bamboo and coloured paper, which ran on wheels. These cars, called " tan-yin," are often fifty feet in height, and are covered with tinsel, flags, and streamers, their different stories being panelled with pictures by Burmese artists, some of which are good and all interesting.

Each car is built by the inhabitants of a different quarter, or neighbouring village, and to honour his disciples the coffin of the dead hpungyi was allowed to rest a certain time on each in turn. While the body was in the car, its proprietors on one side and a rival team on the other engaged in a tug-of-war, good luck to their district through the coming year being the reward of victory ; and it says a good deal for the structure of the cars that they were not pulled to bits, or the coffin thrown out during the struggle.

Encircling the pagoda were two large dragons composed of a framework of wood covered with carpets (offerings to the monastery), the heads, which faced each other, being composed of paper and tinsel, well modelled and *very* fierce, while away to the rear ornate tails of the same material stood defiantly erect.

Alternating with the cars, and overflowing into neighbouring streets and compounds, were temporary zeyats for the hpungyis attending the ceremony, where for a week they reclined on carpets, receiving the offerings of the devout, and generally enjoying a thoroughly lazy time, most of which apparently was spent in chewing betel. The offerings presented were of a most incongruous nature, including brass bedsteads, clocks, spittoons, and betel-boxes, and among others I noticed were two marble statuettes, one being a Greek god, the other Napoleon the Great !

Next to the funeral pyre, over which a lofty canopy of bamboo and paper had been erected, was a long booth occupied by the younger hpungyis and novices, and just before the cremation I witnessed a distribution of gifts to them. Each one received a pillow, a wash basin, a spittoon (as big as a small bucket), a fan, a lamp, a betel-box, and a religous book. A curious combination, but one which, I understand, embraces all their supposed temporal requirements. Each class of articles was the gift of a separate donor, one giving all the fans, another the pillows, etc.

Wandering about enjoying the sights were wild Shans clad in sheepskins and heavy woollen clothing, Chinese, Hindus, and a variety of other types ; processions of boys, some quite naked, dancing and singing to the accompaniment of gongs or pipes, and women of all ranks arrayed in their best, but, alas, their sometimes pretty faces often disfigured with "thanakka," [1] while Indian native police were present to keep order in a crowd far too good-natured to misbehave themselves.

Refreshments were obtainable in sundry cooking shops and stalls, and amusement provided in the form of "pwes" for the elders, and games and a "merry-go-round" for the children. The latter was very primitive, but amusing. I gave the proprietor half a rupee, and told him to give all the children a ride. It was laughable to watch the bystanders, policemen included, catching hold of the youngsters and throwing them *nolens volens* on to the revolving "whirligig." I do not know how far half a rupee was supposed to go, but all the children in the district seemed to have their turn.

Among the other games was one called "thankwin-pyit." This consisted of a long board, covered

---

[1] Thanakka is the bark of a tree, ground to a paste and perfumed, which Burmese women apply to their faces in order to lighten their complexion ; the result, however, far from adding to their beauty, is very often extremely repellent.

with cloth, on which were fixed at intervals coins of different values. For two pies a boy (or girl) would get half a dozen brass rings, which, from a certain distance, were thrown on to the board, and if successful in encircling a coin without touching it, he or she would be paid one of the same value by the proprietor. In this way is the Burmese youth taught to gamble! I noticed, by the way, that all the coins of higher value were fixed quite on the *edge* of the board, where it was almost impossible to obtain a winner! Sometimes this same game is played with knives, spoons, and other articles substituted for the coins.

As is common in all such festivals in Burma, the procession of cars includes grotesque animals of large size; one of these I noticed was a white elephant, considerably over life-size, into which, through a hole in the belly, a man crawled, and with cords caused the trunk to rear, the ears flap, and the tail wag in a most ridiculously realistic manner.

So much for the environments, but to describe the crowd is quite beyond me. Every one was in holiday garb, and I have never before seen so much beauty of texture and colour together as here. A flower garden may suggest the colours, but to these were added the gleam of brown skins, smooth and lovely to look at, hair of the blackest, beautifully dressed, and in the case of the women always adorned with a flower; all of whom, with their quaint walk and pretty gestures, to say nothing of their merry laugh and good-humoured badinage, combined in forming one of the most cheerful and breezily jolly scenes imaginable, and a very anti-thesis to what might have been expected on such an occasion.

The cremation was announced for 9 A.M., but it was after mid-day before the striking of gongs proclaimed the formation of the procession, which, after marching round the square, approached the pyre. It was really a remarkable sight. The coffin, which was gilt, was carried on the shoulders of four men and attended by six hpungyis, each bearing a large silk umbrella fringed with gold. Following came the leading hpungyis and residents in a long procession which was swallowed up in a surging mass of people, pressing forward to salute the priest, or snatch a relic from the pyre.

This was the climax, and, had I known it, the time to leave, as all picturesqueness ceased with the placing of the coffin on the wood. The coffin was broken open with a hatchet, and, after the embalming material had been raked out, turned upside down and the body unceremoniously rolled out upon the logs, then, after it had been covered with sticks, kerosene oil was poured over the whole and set alight.[1]

The moment the flames took hold upon the body the resulting odour was too awful for words! Every one fled, and for half a mile or more, as I drove

[1] Usually the pyre is fired by rockets which run on a guide of canes. These are supplied by the people of the different quarters, in the same manner as the "tan-yin," large wagers being made as to whose rocket shall first set the pile alight. In the instance I have described, however, rockets were not used on account of the confined area in which the ceremony took place.

hurriedly away, was an accompanying stream of Burmans, each with his handkerchief held to his face, escaping from this pestilence which floated heavily on the heated air.

In strange contrast with this modern capital of Burma, with all its gaiety and life, is the silent ruined city of Pagan, whose once glorious epoch reached its zenith at the time of the Norman Conquest of England. Richest in archæological remains, and most interesting of all the old towns in Burma, Pagan, though on the river bank, is the most difficult for tourists to see, the landing-place of Nyaung-u being some miles away from the ancient city, any investigation of which is impossible without at least a brief residence in the neighbour-hood.

There is a good dâk bungalow here, perched on a hill which commands an extensive view of the modern village and the remains of the ancient city, which cover an area of sixteen square miles.

Here again I was fortunate in finding friends to look after me, Mr. Macfarlane, the police commandant, most hospitably putting me up in his bungalow, while Mr. Dunn, Assistant Commissioner, also did everything possible to facilitate my work.

Thanks to the good offices of my friends, the " myook " or native magistrate placed his fine travelling bullock-gharry at my disposal, so that by starting early with provisions and materials for my work, I was able to put in a very full day, until sunset brought an escort of mounted police and a pony for myself for

OLD PAGAN

the homeward journey, a matter of two hours by bullock-gharry, as against half an hour on pony-back.

Passing through the village my daily ride to Pagan was very interesting. The road, hardly defined, is a dusty track crossing a country parched and barren, producing little else but thorns and cactus or desert scrub, and even the little cultivated patches which lie among this desolation only serve to emphasise the poverty of the land.

These cacti which fringe the road and climb among the temples are of many varieties, widely fantastic in their growth, and their fresh green tinged with the red of bursting flower-buds ; thorns and groves of toddy-palms vary the vegetation, and at intervals along the road groups of tamarind-trees give protection to the little rest-houses, whose shade is gratefully sought by many weary pedestrians.

In all directions are pagodas, some still covered with plaster, but more generally of rich terra-cotta brick-work, which harmonises well with the general colour of their surroundings. Enveloping all is a white heat, which makes the vibrating sky appear as cast-iron and the road a gleam of white. Oh, the heat and the dust and the intolerable glare in which, day after day, I had to work ! Yet this very discomfort only added to the romantic picturesqueness which environed this ancient city, dead for nearly a thousand years ! The people and their habitations have long since disappeared, and all that now remains are the twelve hundred or more temples in various stages of ruin, while in place of its once large population are the few priests who occupy the kyaungs, and the six thousand poor villagers of Nyaung-u.

Buddhism was introduced into Pagan early in the eleventh century by Indian refugees from Thaton, and one readily recognises the influence of Indian art upon its temples, most of which have been erected between that era and the end of the thirteenth century. In general these are square-built structures in the form of two or three diminishing terraces, their façades being panelled by low relief pilasters with scroll ornaments over doors and windows, the whole being surmounted by a small cupola. Several, however, are more elegant in form, notably the Ananda temple, whose elongated stupa and innumerable pinnacles give it an airiness and grace wanting in many of the others. Here the Indian influence is marked, though in many of its ornamental features as well as in the surrounding zeyats and kyaungs the Burmese character predominates. In the neighbouring That-pin-yu temple the Indian style is even more pronounced, though built a century later. Both of these are massive buildings, the Ananda being 200 feet square and 168 feet high, while the That-pin-yu is 185 feet square and 201 feet high, both these temples dating from the middle of the eleventh century. The Sula-muni temple, however, built in the thirteenth century and now very ruinous, covers a considerably larger area than either.

There are a great many other temples of various dates, the architecture of which is decidedly Indian in character, though the beautiful Shwe Zigon is purely Burman, as also is the little Bu pagoda which, built right down to the water's edge, is said to be the oldest in the country.

Unlike the "zedi," which is in almost all cases an entirely *solid* structure, most of the temples in Pagan have interior chambers, where, still reposing in their niches, figures of Gaudama remain in placid contemplation of the crumbling walls about them.

Structurally many of these buildings are good. The pointed arch is a common feature both in vaults and doorways, and in many cases, where the first arch is low pitched, others of increasingly acute angles are superimposed to take off the great weight of the upper masonry, for, except for a long corridor and image chamber, most of these huge piles are solid, the staircases leading to the upper terraces, if any, being usually on the outside of the structure. Originally, as in the case of the Ananda, covered with white-washed stucco, time has long since stripped the greater number of this outer coating, exposing brickwork of a peculiarly rich red, in which is revealed an interesting chapter on structural methods.

While most of the temples and theins are entirely ruinous, several are still in excellent repair, and are the resort of pilgrims. Among these is the Ananda, whose huge mass is pierced by lofty corridors, lighted by windows, and to which access is gained by passages leading from four porticoes which face the cardinal points. In each corridor is a large chamber, curiously lit from above, containing colossal upright figures thirty feet in height (not too well carved in wood, and gilded), which represent the four Buddhas of the present cycle. Round these corridors are many smaller niches, also containing Buddhas and other images.

Severely simple in its architecture, the effect of these silent corridors and their commanding effigies is impressive to a degree, and it is difficult to realise that these figures have occupied the same positions unchanged throughout the long centuries which practically represent the history of England !

Outside ornamentation is profuse, one feature being a string-course of panels running round the plinth, composed of plaster and coloured green, in which are figures in low relief representing allegorical and historical subjects ; while in an adjoining chamber the ceiling and walls are profusely decorated with frescoes in fine preservation, depicting principally the various tortures of the Buddhist hell. Inside and out the temple is white-washed, which adds to its feeling of airy grace, especially when seen from a distance or under the spell of moonlight.

It would be quite impossible for me to mention even a small proportion of the interesting remains which cover the plain. Over a thousand temples have been identified, many dating from the ninth century, and there are probably as many more too ruinous to be recognisable. Indeed, so great is their number that "as the pagodas in Pagan" has become a native equivalent for "innumerable."

PLATFORM OF THE SHWE ZIGON PAGODA, PAGAN

Two Capitals

One other pagoda, however, claims attention, and that is the beautiful Shwe Zigon. Situated on the river bank, and built upon a slight eminence, its golden dome is a very commanding object in the landscape. It is approached from the village by a gradually ascending path, paved and enclosed between walls of white stucco. From the south-west is another approach from the road, probably a quarter of a mile in length, and much more distinctive. The entrance is guarded by griffins, and the dromos which is rather winding, is bounded by red-brick walls well built with panels and cornice. At short intervals it is broken by square pilasters, surmounted by griffins and gaudamas alternately ; all are built of brick from which the original stucco has disappeared, but it forms a striking approach to a striking monument.

On the platform are the numerous "tis," votive bowls and sacred trees which stand about the shrines and decorated kyaungs, while the plinth of the zedi is gilded like the dome and enriched by panels of green on which are slightly relieved figure-subjects, such as we have noticed in the Ananda. The picture which faces this page will perhaps give a better idea of the temple precincts than any written description ; the dome, however, does not appear in my drawing, but is of the graceful zedi form, boldly moulded and heavily gilded.

Altogether I was fascinated by the picturesqueness of the place, though strongly impressed with its sense of desolation. I asked a native one day how it was that Pagan had once so many kyaungs and temples and who could have maintained them, the place being now so poor? He replied that they were built long ago, when Pagan was rich and the residence of a king. The king's name was Naw-yat-ta-min-zan, into whose service there entered a hpungyi called Iza-gawna, who had the power of turning iron and lead into gold, and the people in consequence became rich, and had built all these monuments. On the conquest of Pagan by Lower Burma, however, both wealth and population disappeared. The hpungyi died eventually, but, as my informant remarked, "his life is not dead, and people still pray at his pagoda."

CHAPTER X

SOME OTHER TOWNS

NYAUNG-U is a pretty village lying among toddy-palms and tamarinds, and though its narrow roads are usually a cloud of dust from passing gharries it has many attractions; the men are very civil, the women shy but infinitely graceful and attractive in manner, while pretty children run about naked as they play with the dogs and goats.

This is a great centre for the manufacture of red and black lacquer work, quite the best in Burma being produced here. As, however, the chance of direct sale is limited to the wants of occasional steamboat passengers, the people are almost entirely dependent upon the dealers, who evidently do not treat them too liberally. In fact they are desperately poor, and, I am told, cannot even indulge in a full meal of rice, but are obliged to mix millet with it in order to eke out the meal. Yet in spite of this poverty, and many fruitless tramps over miles of dusty road to await the arrival of a steamer, only perhaps to be disappointed of a sale, they are a cheerful community, who try to beautify their lives and their surroundings.

Burma

The houses are, as usual, built largely of bamboo, the matting, of which the walls are composed, being plaited in bold designs, of two or three colours. In front of many are stands of flowers in pots of various kinds, some plain earthenware, others glazed in bright colours. The plants are usually lilies, which, though generally dusty, gleam brightly in the sunlight against the dark background of the gloomy interiors. Surrounding the house is often trellis-work supporting bougainvillea, wisteria, and other flowering creepers, and the footpaths, such as they are, are often shaded by vines.

Except for the shops in which lacquer work[1] is displayed there is not much colour in the articles for sale, food-stuffs and utensils being the principal items ; but on the other hand incidents are plentiful, and, like their more prosperous brethren in more favoured spots, the people are brightly clothed, nor do the women neglect to place a flower in their hair.

[1] The method of lacquer manufacture is interesting. I think I am correct in saying that the ornament or utensil to be lacquered is invariably made of plaited bamboo or other fibre, this foundation of basket work being in itself pretty and ingeniously shaped, and combining strength with elasticity. The whole surface is coated with a resinous varnish, which when dry is rubbed down to a uniformly smooth surface, on a revolving table or lathe. On this black surface is then drawn the design which is to form its decoration, this being done in enamel of whatever colour is to appear, and is laid on with a fine pen or brush, the lines standing up crisp and even above the surface like the wiring of cloisonné work. The whole is then thickly coated with red enamel, and allowed to harden, after which it is again reduced in the lathe until the wearing away of the red coating eventually exposes the lines of the design, and a final varnish completes the process.

BHAMO FROM THE FORT

Some Other Towns

I was very much attracted by the people here, and one day asked the myook if he could procure me two pretty girls as models for a picture which I had in hand. Next day they arrived, and were quite the *ugliest* girls I had seen in Burma ; so do our ideas of beauty vary ! However, as they wore very beautiful clothes, and were neat little things, I was quite pleased to paint them. As models, however, they were hopeless, for the moment they were posed and I began to paint, all their native grace fled and they became rigid as automata. I was hopeless until it occurred to me to pose them *together*, and while pretending to paint one (who immediately became petrified), I was in reality painting the other, who, thinking I was not looking at her, assumed naturally beautiful positions !

Being the daughters of a merchant in the town they were far too high class to accept money, so I gave them each a bundle of cigars and took their photographs as a reward.

A dramatic episode terminated my visit to Pagan. Macfarlane had gone on a tour of inspection, leaving me in sole occupation of his bungalow. Sitting on the verandah after dinner I noticed a fire in the distance, glowing among the palm - trees, and, welcoming any variety in the monotony of a lonely evening, I strolled down to the village to see what was happening.

During my ten minutes' walk to the seat of the fire, which was evidently extending, I met hurrying groups of excited people carrying away their beds and furniture to the river bank for safety, and as I neared the spot

Burma

I found it was evidently a big blaze. Though terribly sorry for the sufferers, I have never seen anything finer as a display, ten or twelve houses being alight, the blaze shining on gilded pagodas and through the dark palm groves, while the heat was such that I could not approach without screening my face with my hands. The fire was spreading quickly, and seemed likely to burn the whole place down ; and the flames, leaping across the street or dropping like molten metal from the eaves, spread in all directions. No one appeared to be doing anything, the police contenting themselves with patrolling the place with bayonets fixed. I felt really indignant at the apathy displayed, and through an interpreter I got some men together and started to grapple with the situation. The fire was progressing at the rate of a house every five minutes, so, telling the people to remove their belongings, we began to demolish the houses some little way down the street as an interceptor. No one seemed to dispute my authority, and it was almost amusing the way in which the crowd seemed to enjoy the demolition of another's property !

Meanwhile palms and other trees had caught fire, and the flames threatened the handsome group of pagodas and kyaungs which was the pride of the village. Fortunately the wind changed before they were seriously endangered, and the demolished buildings effectually arrested the progress of flames in the other direction, but not before twenty-five homes had been completely destroyed. It was certainly a great catastrophe, though the people took it for the most part with apathetic indifference. One poor woman alone became quite crazy and stood, crying and shouting, until she was almost caught by the fire, before some one dragged her away from her burning domicile.

I was much amused by one man who was comfortably seated on his doorstep smoking a cheroot, and entirely indifferent to the excitement which surrounded him. His house, however, was one which had to be sacrificed, and his disgusted expression, as we began to pull the place down and his neighbours to remove his goods, was truly comical. It was not so much anger or distress at the destruction of his home, but simple annoyance at being so rudely disturbed in the enjoyment of his smoke!

Many of the women were engaged in bringing water from the river, which they did in small chatties, strolling quietly to and from the scene of the fire, then waiting, chattering, until it would occur to somebody to take the pot from off their head and pour the water on the flames! An absolutely futile operation, but it kept them occupied and out of the way.

I was engaged in this way until after midnight, and in spite of my sympathy with the sufferers hugely enjoyed the fillip of this exciting experience. I had certain doubts, however, as to the legality of my action in ordering the destruction of so much property, but was relieved to find afterwards that Mr. Dunn, the local representative of authority, had been engaged in precisely similar operations on the other side of the conflagration.

Burma

The following morning before leaving I visited the scene of the fire, where, over an acre or more of still smoking timbers and hot ashes, strewn with innumerable water-pots and cooking utensils apparently none the worse for their firing, roamed dozens of these homeless people searching among the débris for lost treasures. No one, I heard, was burnt, and those whose homes had been destroyed had all been accommodated by their neighbours, and even before I had left, life was again going on as happily and placidly as if nothing had occurred.

If my departure from Nyaung-u had been marked by disaster, my return to Prome was ushered in with festivities, for on arrival I discovered my host, Mr. Litchfield, assisted by several young ladies, busily engaged in transforming his usually severe drawing-office into a ball-room ! Naturally I was pressed into the service, and an unlimited supply of palms, bamboos, lanterns, and trophies being available, the result of our combined efforts was distinctly successful. The greatest triumph, however, was the decoration of the large tent which served as a supper-room, which was entirely the work of the ladies ; and, a piano having at considerable trouble been procured from Rangoon, everything appeared to be in perfect readiness for the event.

With the arrival of the guests, however, arose a problem. The whole social circle of Prome numbered less than thirty, and the question as to who should supply the music became acute. None of the men could play, and the ladies were too few to be spared, and a fiasco threatened! Happily our host, among other provision for our amusement, had obtained a gramophone and an ample supply of records, so that, instead of the piano, the musical programme was furnished by waltzes and quadrilles as rendered by the best military bands of Europe, and the dance was a huge success.

Under such pleasant circumstances was I introduced to Prome society, and even if its circle *was* a limited one, its amenities suffered not one whit through lack of numbers; and in many ways Prome stands out prominent in all the virtues which are embraced in the single term " hospitality."

Here was a nice little club, built on the river bank, well finished and well managed, a billiard-room for the men, and for the ladies the best room in the house, admission to which was not denied ourselves. Indeed one of the most charming features of club life in Burma is this universal provision for the wants of the ladies, whose comfort and need of amusement are as carefully considered as those of the men, and it need hardly be added how greatly their presence adds to the social attraction of the club itself.

Built out into the water was a stage on which we would sit and watch the after-glow spread behind the opposite hills, pretty by day, but in the twilight full of romance, as their bases, lost in gloom, merged in the deep reflections of the silent river. These pleasant evenings constantly recur to my mind, when, after the great heat of the day, we would enjoy the cool of the evening, and witness the slow transition from the strongly opposed light and shade of sunset to the silvery effulgence of the moon.

Prome is a picturesque town of considerable size, having a population of some 30,000 people, and it appeared to me to be one of the best built in the country. The streets are wide, well laid and wooded; and the houses, which are frequently of two stories, are large and more solidly constructed than in the majority of Burmese country towns. Pagodas of various styles and ages are frequent, and its local life is interesting.

Though the offensive ngapi is perhaps its principal trade, it has been famous for the manufacture of gold lacquer, which, though ornate and handsome, does not please me as much as the more simple black-and-red work of Pagan. It has a handsome church, and the bungalows of residents and officials are comfortable and surrounded by pretty gardens. But it is insanitary to a degree, and cannot well be healthy in its present condition. In the middle of the town are tanks, stagnant and covered with water plants, hidden below which lie the usual sacred fish or turtles. Beside the poorer roads, and crossed by wooden bridges which give access to the houses, are open drains, often without any fall whatever, and forming pools on which the children sail their little toy boats or paddle at their brinks. Consequently Prome is unhealthy, and I was not surprised to hear that fever was a constant visitant.

Some Other Towns

I escaped fever, but had my first experience of prickly-heat, and of the two I think I prefer the fever. However, I had not much time to consider ailments, with so many interesting scenes to occupy my attention. Every street corner was a picture ; picturesque houses buried in handsome trees, below which were the pumps and fountains surrounded by pretty groups of children or their elders ; here a primitive ropewalk on wheels ; there a lad kite-flying, his little sister sitting beside him wondering how it is done ; or, again, a group of half-naked youths playing "chinlon" or other games.

Chinlon is the Burmese form of football, and is the national game. The name means "round basket," and the "chinlon" is really a ball of about six inches in diameter formed of plaited rattans. The game is played by several youths or men who stand in a circle a few feet apart, and the ball having been thrown into play, the one nearest to whom it falls kicks it up into the air with the instep, knee, or side of the foot, the effort being to keep it in the air as long as possible, and without losing possession of the ball. A fancy stroke is to turn right round as the ball falls and kick it with the sole of the foot, though the elbows, head, or any part of the body except hands and toes may be used. While playing no one leaves his place, but waits until the ball falls within his reach, when he in turn endeavours to retain its possession. This is a very pretty game to watch, and the skill of the performers is often surprising.

The great interest of Prome, however, is centred

in its pagoda, the Shwe-Tsan-Daw, one of the largest in Lower Burma, and in many respects even more beautiful than the Shwe Dagon itself.

The pagoda stands on a hillock 138 feet in height, and overlooks the river. As usual it is approached by four covered stairways of brick, guarded by large leogryphs of stucco, behind which rise the carved roofs of the ascent. At the entrance a large notice-board bears this inscription in English and Burmese, "No one permitted to wear shoes in this pagoda but Englishmen and Asiatic Europeans," an example of baboo English which recalls another where, in a petition, the writer picturesquely describes himself as "a man without a head (employer), and whose belly is fed with debts"!

The ascent, which is as usual frequented by blind musicians and other mendicants and forms a bazaar, terminates in a gallery surmounted by a handsome pyathat, beneath which are placed many large Buddhas, coloured and gilded, all in the usual attitude of meditation. Passing through this, the platform is reached, which, though relatively small in area, is more than usually rich in carved zeyats and gilded shrines. In the centre the great dome itself, 180 feet in height and particularly graceful in form, rises from a square base of many moulded courses, each corner of which is crowned by a lesser pagoda or cupola. Running round the plinth, but joined together so as to form a continuous wall, are eighty-three carved and gilded niches, each containing a figure of Buddha, and each

PRAYER ON THE PAGODA PLATFORM. PROME.

surmounted by a cupola of different design. The whole mass is gilt and enclosed in an ornamental railing of metallic green ; while from the summit of the great zedi, and from every lesser pinnacle, bells and cymbals swing and tinkle merrily from the golden "tis" which crown them. The effect is gorgeous, and as no shrines have been built on to the pagoda itself, its whole beautiful symmetry and proportion may be properly appreciated.

On the outer edge of this platform are a large number of zeyats and shrines, among which are innumerable bells which hang between their coloured uprights, "tis" of silk or gilded metal and "ta-gun-daing," whose streamers float softly in the breeze.

Many of the details of ornament are very fine, the perforated carvings of the eaves or cornices are exceptionally delicate, as are the screens of carved teak which arch the spaces between the supporting columns of the roofs. Glass mosaic and tile-work in bright colours form panels in the shrines, or encase pillars which are otherwise painted or overlaid with gold. The whole scheme of colour is a sumptuous play of vermilion and gold, with an occasional accent of vivid green or smoke-blackened altar as a foil.

In and about all this beauty of ornament were the figures of the people, while numbers of squirrels chased and gambolled among its pinnacles and spires. I made no attempt to paint what I have described, it was too hopelessly bewildering ; but, searching out the simplest of its corners, I was fain to content myself

with the less ornate beauty of such " bits " as the one
I reproduce.

From the edge of the platform are splendid views
in all directions, that across the Irrawaddy valley being
the most striking ; while all around, and climbing the
little hill upon which the pagoda stands, trees of various
growths effectually separate it from the busy town
below, as though jealously safeguarding the jewelled
temple they surround.

Of another kind is Thayetmyo, " mango city." Once
a frontier town and a military station of great importance,
Thayetmyo has fallen upon evil days, and in place of a
former large establishment its garrison at the time of my
visit consisted of but half a battalion of British troops, and
two native regiments.   Everywhere were signs of decay;
large barracks and military lines were deserted and falling
into disrepair, and for want of tenants, officers' quarters
and handsome bungalows were allowed to go to ruin.[1]

The town, however, has many attractions in its
shady avenues, wooded tanks, and charming environs ;
and the people, with characteristic cheerfulness, decline
to be despondent, and would convey to the casual
observer the idea that they are still an important and
prosperous community !   Certainly the bazaars are
large and well attended, the country and river trade
probably being as extensive as formerly.   Many of
the shops are extremely good, and most of the stores
used in my first jungle trip were purchased here.
Some of the tradesmen appear to be enterprising, and

[1] The garrison has since been entirely withdrawn.

over one shop I read the sign, " E. Cheap Jack & Co.," which struck me as being quite up-to-date. But, all said and done, Thayetmyo is a place of the past, and its silent fort, grass-grown and gunless, speaks eloquently of its fall from high estate.

In and about the town are many pretty roads, some wide and grassy, and often the scene of gorgeous religious pageants ; others are narrow and winding, overhung with trees and creepers which effectually conceal the native huts, and having the appearance of country lanes. Strolling up one of these lanes one afternoon I came upon an open space, in which a football match was in progress between a team of the Border Regiment and one composed entirely of Burmans. I joined the large crowd assembled to witness the match, and was struck by the energy with which the Burmans, who played barefooted, entered into the game, upon which of course the crowd was betting freely.

Close beside the dâk bungalow, shaded by mango-trees, is an interesting group of pagodas, one of which is a particularly fine example of plaster-work ; the river banks also furnished many a good subject for a painter, and I wish I could have spent a longer time here. As it was, I thoroughly enjoyed my short time at Thayetmyo as the guest of Captain Moffat and the mess of the King's Own Scottish Borderers ; nor will I soon forget the charming entertainment and Christmas tree given by the officers to the children of the station, in which I had the pleasure of participating.

Though in their general features one Burmese town

Burma

is much like another, I cannot leave this subject without a reference to Bhamo, which differs essentially from any other I have visited.

Far away in the north and close to the frontier of China, its characteristics are more Chinese than Burman, the bazaar, in which is a most interesting joss-house, being almost entirely so. The population, however, is of a very mixed character, as I had an early opportunity of judging.

I had just arrived at the fort, where I was the guest of Major and Mrs. Bernard, and with them I attended the garrison sports, which were given that afternoon on the parade ground. It was a most interesting sight, and every event was keenly contested. There were tent-pegging for the troopers, tugs-of-war and obstacle races for the regiments, and indescribably funny flat races in which the competitors were of all ages and nationalities, from senior Non-Coms. of native regiments to wonderfully clad Indian servants or half-naked Chinese children. Earnest rivalry on the part of the competitors was blended with hilarious good-humour among the cosmopolitan crowd of onlookers, which embraced every race I have mentioned in this volume, and probably many more besides.

In view of its hybrid character one would hardly expect to find much of purely Burman interest here, though several monuments are noteworthy, notably the bell-shaped stupa of the pagoda in my picture, which was the only one of its kind I saw in Burma, and is probably unique. For the rest Burmese and

THE RIVER AT PROME MORNING MISTS RISING

Some Other Towns

Chinese jostle and intermix, each partaking a little of the character of the other.

It is in its surroundings that Bhamo is most interesting. The midan, where I witnessed a polo match, is fifteen feet under water in the rains, and instead of equestrian sports, fishermen in dug-outs drag their nets with profit.

To the north is a pretty ride by wooded lanes and through a picturesque Assamese village to the Taiping River, on whose bank are the remains of the ancient Shan city of Tsan-pan-ago, of which, however, little now remains but interesting ruins of moated walls and pagodas well worth exploring, and which, as is always the case in Burma, nature has beautified with an envelopment of trees and flowering shrubs.

Most interesting of all, however, is the "road to China"—a broad highway cut through virgin forest to the frontier, bordered by forest trees and jungle, and along which pass numerous caravans of Chinese bound for Bhamo : strange wild folk, and strangely clad, who wear a curious woven yoke or collar, which, with a rope across the forehead, enables them to support the surprising loads they carry.

We drove a considerable distance along this road, and I was charmed with its alternation of lofty trees and pretty clearings, in which were farmsteads strongly reminiscent of home. Miles away from Bhamo we found a little booth by the roadside where, among other creature comforts, were sold American " Railway Cigarettes" and Japanese safety matches, while all round were thickets infested by tiger and leopard. I was told of one tiger, a confirmed man-eater, whose lair was here, which had adopted the habit of watching the caravans pass and picking off the last man, whose companions in front were often quite unaware of what was happening. Finally his depredations became so numerous that a hunt was organised and he was eventually shot.

On our return home by way of the " circular road," also cut through the jungle encircling the town, when passing a certain point, Major Bernard called in his dogs, which had been running alongside, and took them into the cart beside us, telling me that it was not an uncommon occurrence for pets to be snapped up by lurking tigers or panthers just thereabouts. This, however, was the general, if not the only, drive available for the ladies and children of the garrison !

CHAPTER XI

A MONTH ON THE LASHIO LINE

" WELL, I have seen your line, and I call it sheer impertinence ! " was the comment of a fair American upon that section of the Burma railways which connects Mandalay with Lashio, a village on the borders of China, and situated in the extreme north-east corner of the Northern Shan States.

Through the courtesy of the agent, Captain Kincaid, R.E., who most kindly placed an inspection car at my disposal for the purpose, I was afforded the opportunity of making intimate acquaintance with the section, which, by repeated surmounting of almost insuperable engineering difficulties, would seem to justify the opinion I have quoted.

My stores of provisions, fuel, etc., having been put on board, I joined the car overnight, sleeping in the station in readiness for an early start, my car being attached to the train timed to leave at 6 A.M., and just as the sun rose behind the Shan hills on the east we steamed out of the station.

It was a lovely morning, the mists lying on the

plain and hiding the base of the hills, whose tops stood out sharp and clear against the sunrise. On the west the pinnacles and domes of Amarapura were softly white among the foliage, and here at last I was able for the first time to obtain a real impression of the Arracan pagoda, whose gilded mass, broken by innumerable pinnacles, gleamed softly through the sun-suffused haze in which the waning moon was setting. Turning sharply to the left, the line headed for the hills, running through fertile fields broken by winding rivulets and groups of trees, the whole swathed in a mantle of haze which slowly succumbed to the growing power of the sun.

At Tônbo we stopped to attach another engine before attacking the almost perpendicular hill-side which at Sêdaw seemed to effectually bar our farther progress. Here the stationmaster came to ask me if I had any objection to being detached from the train and remaining until a goods train in the evening could take me on. Asking the reason, I was told that the engines could only carry a certain weight up the steep gradient, and that my car made the train just one coach too heavy. As I had given ample notice at Mandalay, and I was not sure that the same difficulty would not arise with the succeeding train, I insisted on going on, and only upon restarting found that, in order to oblige me, a whole carriage full of third-class passengers had been detached and shunted into a siding. I was very sorry for this, but as my time was valuable I felt I could not reproach myself too much, and I do not doubt that the unlucky

IN THE BAZAAR. BHAMO

A Month on the Lashio Line

Burmans left behind had a sufficiency of light-heartedness and philosophy with which to face the situation !

Any sense of meanness vanished as we slowly climbed the precipitous hill in the early morning light, the scene being one I would not have missed to oblige a hundred natives ! It was one of the things I had come to see, and I saw it and was glad !

By a series of reversing stations, up gradients of 1 in 25, we slowly zigzagged up the face of the mountain, while below the broad plain of Ava rose slowly into the sky, a sea of paddy land and jungle which disappeared into blue distance, and at our feet, far below, lay the little station we had left. Along the foot hills wound a sluggish stream, and through the distant haze peeped the pink tops of the Sagaing hills. Mounting still higher, Mandalay hill appeared above an intervening spur of the mountain whose broad shadow stretched half a mile across the plain, while like a silver ribbon the Irrawaddy gleamed through the mist which still obscured the horizon.

Reaching the crest, the line wound along a ridge bordered by deep valleys filled with trees, glorious in autumn tints which ranged from the crimson and scarlet of the dhak and cotton-tree to the pale yellow of the bamboo.

Still ascending through an indaing forest, we presently reached a high plateau covered with jungle, in which were a few cultivated patches ; this again was succeeded by another rise, clothed with forest, through which ran sparkling streams which scored the mountain sides, exposing rocks and boulders overhung with creepers, among which the clear water danced and leapt in a succession of waterfalls. As elsewhere in Burma, the vegetation was luxuriant, but, owing to the elevation, of a slightly different character from what I have described elsewhere. Tall grasses, like pampas grass, alternated with lilies ten feet high, and among other flowering shrubs was one much like a pomegranate, while the kidney-leaved bauhinia, whose blossoms resemble the pelargonium, hung in clusters above the trailing convolvulus. Among the trees also were many new growths, including the wild plum, and at intervals clumps of papaya marked the place where at one time the nomadic Shans had made a home.

It had been my intention to stop at Maymu, 3600 feet above sea-level, and the Simla of Burma. From the station, however, the little town with its trim bungalows and military lines seemed to offer so little pictorial inducement that I decided to push on to the Goekteik gorge, one of the principal objectives of my journey.

Passing many pretty villages, such as Hsum-Hsai, and little hamlets and pagodas half hidden among the bamboo clumps, we again wound our way uphill and downhill through gorgeous mountain and forest scenery, until, reaching a summit of 3000 feet of elevation, a quick run downhill over a winding track brought us to the Goekteik, where at 2.30 P.M. my car was detached from the train and run into a siding.

Generally the line had been closely girt by jungle

and forest; my little siding, however, could not have been more fortunately placed, as here the land fell away in front of me to the ravine below, so giving me an almost uninterrupted view of the splendid panorama before me.

Right and left stretched a winding valley, a mile or more in width, surrounded by high hills clad to their crests with vegetation. Behind me on the hill-side hung the little station, while from my feet the sloping ground, covered with jungle of many growths, swept gently to the edge of a ravine which cleft the valley to a depth of several hundred feet. Through this ravine flowed a rapid river, which at one point entered a natural tunnel which pierced a barrier of rock 400 feet in height. On the farther side high bluffs of limestone, strongly marked by streaks of red and yellow, rose precipitously from the river, perhaps to the height of 1000 feet or so, they in turn being capped by tree-clad downs.

This point presented the greatest engineering problem in the construction of the line, which is here carried by a graceful trestle bridge across the valley and gorge to the bluffs beyond, where, by a series of tunnels and tortuous windings along the hill-sides, it eventually reaches the summit of the downs, many hundred feet above the level of the bridge itself.

It is not easy by description to convey an adequate idea of the difficulties surmounted in carrying out the work, and though figures do not usually form attractive reading, I am tempted to use them here.

Burma

The abutments and foundations for the trestles were prepared by the Railway Company, an American firm of engineers being charged with the erection of the bridge itself, whose total length of 2260 feet is carried on fifteen lattice-work trestles. The highest of these trestles is 320 feet, and rests upon the natural bridge of rock which spans the Chungzoun River, 825 feet below rail-level. In its construction about 4300 tons of iron and steel were used, including over 1,000,000 rivets, its entire cost being about £113,200. The cost of painting alone is enormous, being about £800, and the surface painted 401,500 square feet.

These figures will give some little idea of the magnitude of the work, which, though carried on in the wildest surroundings of mountain and forest, and notwithstanding the fact that every pound of metal used in its construction had to be shipped from New York, was completed in the incredibly short time of nine months.[1]

Turning from the material to the pictorial, the scenery was splendid, especially when at sunset the warm light glowed upon the rocky projections of the valley, and the creeping shadows lent an additional depth of colour to the rich vegetation. From the comfortable and well-built rest-house erected by the Railway Company a pathway led through the dense jungle to the edge of the ravine, where a zigzag path cut in the face of the rock descended to the river bed itself.

[1] The general design of the bridge is the work of Sir A. M. Rendel & Co. of London, the detail plans and construction being carried out by the Pennsylvania Steel Company.

A Month on the Lashio Line

This pathway is very beautiful. Heavily shaded by forest trees, in which squirrels and lemurs play, a pleasant green tone softens the light falling upon grey stone or tree-trunks ; from every projection as well as from the boughs hang trailing plants, and ferns and flowers spring from the crevices of rocks whose rugged contours are softened by mosses and brightly coloured lichens.

At every point of vantage seats have been placed, from which are views of extreme loveliness, and every turn in the path reveals some new charm of colour or effect. As the lower level is reached the air is cold and damp, and the dripping rocks are covered with clinging plants whose names I know not, while huge lily leaves mix with the lighter foliage which partly screens the river from view. It is a series of pictures of almost unnatural beauty, which finds a strong note of contrast in the dark-mouthed and sombre cavern in which the river loses itself.

From the shingle bed of the river the scene is very impressive. Almost perpendicular cliffs surround you as the eye slowly mounts to the point from which, far beyond the ordinary angle of vision, the delicate tracery of the viaduct rises high into the air without offending.

Truly the Goekteik gorge is an amazing sight tempting to the use of superlatives, and one which no visitor to Mandalay should fail to see.

Here I naturally settled down to work, though with little hope of realising the half of its bewildering beauty. Months rather than days might be spent upon any one of its charming pictures, but the artist on tour must be content if happily he accomplishes even a semblance to the spirit of the scene which enthrals him.

Night fell early in the dark ravine, and the toilsome ascent of twenty minutes to my camp, 900 feet above, was through deepening gloom, and frequently under the escort of panthers, which in twos and threes hovered round me. On reaching the station I would find my boy busy cooking dinner on a wood fire built beside the line, and no matter where I was, he somehow always managed to prepare a dainty meal, for which he never failed to write a " menu." [1] Here is the facsimile of one of these :—

DINNR.

Browen sup.	Roast mutton.
Fish cod roes.	Sweetbread.
Mutton pancaek.	Cabnet puding.
Brisciut baick.	

As it was my home during the expedition, a description of the car may be of interest. In size it was about the same as an ordinary coach, the half being fitted up as a combined sitting and bed room. The bed was roomy and comfortable, and the several easy chairs it contained left ample room for dining table and seats. All round the walls were cupboards and lockers, so that everything in use might be easily stowed away, and electric light and fans added luxury to comfort.

[1] Among other dishes, my servant on several occasions gave me boiled bamboo shoots, which, though slightly astringent, were palatable and a welcome substitute for vegetable food.

A Month on the Lashio Line

The supply of electricity was generated "en route" and stored in batteries capable of maintaining a week's supply, and should, as occasionally happened, a prolonged stay at any point exhaust the reserves, a run of 100 miles attached to any passing train was sufficient replenishment. Adjoining the saloon was a roomy bathroom and lavatory ; beyond were the servants' room, kitchen, and store-room. In reality it was a comfortable *maisonnette* on wheels, and as the end of the saloon had windows, I always arranged to be attached to the rear of the train, so that I could sit comfortably in a chair and enjoy the whole sweep of the landscape uninterruptedly. Only one thing I missed, which was a *fire*. The nights were very cold, and I frequently found ice on the puddles in the morning, but during the day the heat was often great. I was not careful, I am afraid, to note temperatures very accurately, but I find these figures in my notes for the 4th of February :—8 A.M., 38° F. ; noon, 82° ; 6 P.M., 64°, these of course being taken indoors.

The morning fogs were very heavy, covering the highest hills, and were damp and bitterly cold, and I found it necessary to take a brisk walk along the line to set my circulation going until at about 9 A.M. the wind and sun finally dissipated the fog. Its effect as it slowly melted was interesting, little glimpses of rock and trees appearing in patches, sometimes lit by a gleam of sunlight in wonderful contrast to the even greyness of the mist ; and I remember one curious illusion of a man, seemingly headless, walking

towards me, the colour of his turban being the same
as that of the fog, in which it could not be noticed.

The railway line here forms the only high road, and
is freely used by the Shans, whose quaint costume and
enormous grass hats lent interest to the landscape.
I found these Shans very quiet, intelligent people, and
I was frequently surrounded by them when painting.
While at work one day upon a study of a ficus-encircled
eng-tree two women stopped to look at what I was
doing. "He is painting that tree," said one, point-
ing to the tree before me. "No," replied the other,
"it is that one with the creeper on it," which was
correct (as of course I was seated sideways to my
subject), and the old woman had compared my sketch
with the surroundings. I felt pleased to think that
when all these trees are so similar I had caught the
character of this particular one in a way which appealed
to the intelligence of a native utterly ignorant of art.

I regretted very much that I was unable to speak
to the natives, whose quiet demeanour and respectful-
ness appealed to me, and though my servant understood
Burmese, the Shan dialect proved a difficulty to him.
That they are nice in their nature I think the following
will show. A girl, the sister of the stationmaster's
wife, every day climbed down the steep declivity to
the river, returning almost immediately. I asked her
what she found to attract her so much down there, and
she explained that in the cavern grew a beautiful white
flower, a water-plant, which she gathered daily in order
to decorate the little station-house. These Shan girls,

IN THE GOEKTEIK GORGE

A Month on the Lashio Line

by the way, are often very pretty, and have really rosy cheeks, and, except for their costume, might often pass for English rustics.

From Goekteik to Hsipaw, my next headquarters, the journey was much as I have already described, and as we mounted higher into the heart of the Shan hills the country seemed to expand itself into an immense sea of tree-clad undulations. The exuberance of the vegetation is extraordinary ; every inch of ground supports some form of growth, each elbowing the other for space in which to reach the light and air. Should a tree die, a dozen creepers fight for its possession, while its topmost branches are crowned with orchids. In many places are clearings, where, in made terraces flooded with irrigation water, Shans and Shan-tilôks [1] are planting paddy, their little hamlets being almost lost to sight amidst the vegetation, from which at times rises a long bamboo flagstaff erected as a " tagundaing " to mark a holy place. Cart roads and gharries are almost unknown in this district, but in their place large herds of pack ponies browse upon the hill-sides, or, heavily laden, wind their devious way through the forest.

Such in general character was the country in which I was working, a rich succession of forest land interspersed with pastoral incident, fascinating in the extreme, but difficult of description. To me, however, this was a period of extreme loneliness, which the very superabundance of natural beauty only served to intensify. This was especially the case when, my day's

[1] Half Shans, half Chinese.

work over, the mellow afterglow suffused the hushed landscape with its mysterious light, and all nature seemed to be looking westward, as though desiring to follow the sun in its course, a longing my heart often echoed in a feeling of intense home-sickness.

My arrival at Hsipaw was a welcome break in the somewhat solitary nature of my existence, and as trains from this point to Lashio only run on alternate days, I thoroughly enjoyed the relative activity of its life during the day and a night spent there. Very pleasant too was the unexpected meeting with Messrs. Sterne and Kindersley, who were returning to Rangoon after a visit to the Great Eastern Mines, two days' journey to the north, and of which I will have more to say later.

While we were enjoying our dinner, sounds of music reached us from the station, followed by a personal invitation from the stationmaster to honour a function with our presence. It appeared that among the other passengers waiting to proceed was a strolling company of Indian Nautch players and dancers, who were giving a performance in that portion of the station buildings reserved for third-class passengers. This consisted of a large roofed compound enclosed by an iron railing, which on our arrival we found to be packed by an appreciative native audience. From the roof all available lanterns had been hung and the floor covered with clean white sand, the centre forming a ring for the performers, into which the three easy chairs placed for ourselves somewhat intruded.

A Month on the Lashio Line

We were received with acclamation, more especially from the performers, who no doubt anticipated "backsheesh," and then the entertainment proceeded. I had not before witnessed an Indian Nautch, and was more pleased with the performance than I had expected. The music, in which tom-toms figured largely, was really pretty, and I should think capable of English notation. The dancing girls, handsome and richly dressed, performed well, the dance being graceful and accompanied by a song of strange fascination. One by one the dancers relieved each other, continuing the same song which consisted of one motif, rhythmic and flowing with a decided melody, but which was never resolved, repeating itself interminably. The words of the song were, as usual, immoral, but I could not help feeling how beautiful a "fantasia" might have been constructed from it by a capable musician.

Next morning at 7.30 I left for Lashio, the scenery differing entirely from what I had already passed through. For its entire length the line followed the windings of the Myit-ngé or "Little River," a stream abounding in falls and rapids, above which rose forest-clad mountains of from 2000 to 3000 feet in height. Though to all appearance a likely place for fish, I learned that during the construction of the line the river near Hsipaw had been so persistently "dynamited" by the work-people that the fish had deserted these waters, and had never returned. Higher up the stream, however, the large number of otters frequenting its waters, and the presence of fishing weirs at every hamlet on its banks, would seem to show that the river is still well stocked in places.

These fishing weirs are interesting, and are usually of two kinds. In level stretches of the river the weir, composed of bamboo wicker, is built in the form of a large oval, having at each end a narrow entrance through which the fish enter, and which, becoming confused, they are unable to find again. Where falls occur, however, the inside edge of the ledge of rock is fenced from bank to bank, and the fish, unable to pass the obstruction, lie in the slack water behind, and are picked up by hand or basket. In many cases I noticed that in the centre was built a raised staging, shaded by a thatched roof, beneath which sat the fisherman, who, spider-like, watched the line of fencing on either side ready to pounce upon the fish the moment they struck the barricade.

In several places, close beside the line, were precipitous crags of limestone, covered with trees and literally alive with monkeys, which, however, were by no means common in the more open country; new growths also appeared in the shape of the areca-nut palm, purple wisteria, crimson daisies, and a flower which I took to be the familiar "love lies bleeding."

Birds abounded, including bulbul, jay, and peacock, and near Lashio I saw many nests of the weaver bird.

At Lashio I had a rather amusing experience. Provisions had run low, and being badly in need of chickens, eggs, and butter, I sent my servant into the village to make the necessary purchases. He returned saying that the "stupid Shans" would sell him nothing, as they knew it was for the "sahib" who would kill the chickens! Food had to be obtained somehow, so I appealed to the stationmaster, who rather impolitely declined to assist me.[1] Finally invoking the aid of a stalwart native policeman, he and my boy went on a foraging expedition and simply *stole* what was required. This was the first time in which I had ever compounded a felony, but I felt justified in this case, more particularly when later the outraged owners, who came clamouring round my car, retired well pleased with the perhaps over-liberal compensation paid them.

For some reason the railway stops short of Lashio and the Chinese frontier by some miles, and though no doubt the Government has some sufficient reason for prohibiting its farther extension, it seemed to me that the completion of the section could not fail to be commercially advantageous. A large trade is already carried on with China—pickled tea, onions, ginger, and other commodities being brought in, in exchange for Burmese and British products; but the trade is hampered by the obligation on the people of carrying their goods upon their backs, often for long distances, before the railway is struck. These straggling lines of figures, curiously attired and armed, added much to the picturesqueness of local life, but I could not but feel

---

[1] In all fairness I must add that this was the only case of incivility I ever experienced at the hands of any of the railway servants, who were invariably most attentive, and, particularly in the case of Mr. Millar, stationmaster at May-mu, put themselves to considerable trouble in order to make my journey comfortable.

that here was the foundation of a trade capable of rapid development, but which we were doing little to encourage.

The immediate vicinity of Lashio offered no special pictorial attraction, and I therefore returned to Manpwe, whose grand succession of waterfalls shares with the Goekteik gorge the honours of the line for magnificence of scenic effect.

Here for many miles the river is broken by innumerable cascades, which at a point some five miles below the station culminate in a series of fifteen falls, ranging in height from 50 to 120 feet, by which, in single leaps over terraces of yellow rock, the river drops many hundreds of feet in level. Between the falls are deep pools, whose vividly green water gleams transparent as an emerald amongst the forest trees now in their autumn foliage. The coloration is splendid, and the whole effect of the scene impressive to a degree. From no point are all these falls visible at the same time, but with great judgment the Railway Company has built a dâk bungalow in a position to command a view of what is perhaps the finest group of all, and ladders and paths cut in the precipitous rock face lead to otherwise inaccessible points from which nearer views of individual falls are obtainable.

Though completed structurally, the bungalow was not ready to receive visitors while I was there, and as no siding was available for my car it remained at the station, trolleys pushed by Indian coolies being provided by the Company to take me to and from my work.

A Month on the Lashio Line

These trolley rides in the early morning were most exhilarating. The line descends in steep gradients of 1 in 40 to 1 in 25, winding in and out of the spurs of the mountains in abrupt curves round which we swung at a speed which almost took one's breath away. Indeed the pace was at times almost alarming, and had the trolley jumped the rails at any point, or the brakes refused to act when required, the consequences would have been unpleasant to contemplate. As it was, the daily journey of five miles was covered in little over a quarter of an hour, and fortunately without mishap.

In contrast with this brief period of excitement, the rest of the day was spent alone, amid surroundings the grandeur of which gradually overcame its mere beauty and often became oppressive.

It is difficult in a sketch to convey any real idea of the *scale* of a scene in which everything from the forest trees to the falls themselves was proportionally large, but, as hour after hour, and day after day I worked here, I seemed momentarily to become more insignificant as the *bigness* of it all possessed me ; and, in spite of the glorious light and colour which might well have induced a spirit of cheerfulness, for the second time during this journey I felt utterly and painfully alone.

There is always, I think, a peculiar impressiveness, a sense of majesty and power in rushing water, and these magnificent falls, thundering as they fell, overawed me more than others I have seen of greater height and volume. This was particularly the case when, climbing along the rugged paths in the rocks, I would stand almost spellbound below the cliff over which the river poured splendidly into the deep pool at my feet, again to vanish into space over the edge of a succeeding abyss. The perpetual noise of running water also has a numbing effect upon the brain, especially when, as here, it is with you daily to the exclusion of all other sounds ; and it was with a sense of extreme relief that at sunset, the tension of work relaxed, I would return slowly and toilsomely to camp.

Pushing the trolley uphill was hard work for my coolies, and in contrast with the quick run down to the falls, the return journey often occupied an hour and a half, so that when possible I arranged to pick up a ballast train, then filled with engineers and workmen returning from their work some distance down the valley.

The permanent way of the line requires constant watching, for owing to its heavy gradients, the usual "creep" of a line in the direction of its traffic is here exaggerated to an unusual degree, and instead of the proper interval always left between rails to allow for expansion, the downward slide of metals and sleepers causes them to impinge closely, which if allowed to continue beyond a certain point would result in a "buckling" of the rails and inevitable disaster to any passing train. The I.P.W. of this section therefore has a busy time, and is constantly employed in inspecting and reballasting the line, which is kept in wonderful order, and even round the sharpest curves the rolling

THE MAN-JWE FALLS

A Month on the Lashio Line

stock travels smoothly. The navvies employed are largely Indian, and I was interested in watching them at work. Two men whom I noticed were engaged in packing up the sleepers by hoeing in the metalling and ramming it underneath them with a long-handled hoe ; with great ingenuity labour was divided between them, one exerting all his energy in a sharp backward haul upon the handle, while his "mate," squatting upon the ground, controlled its effect by guiding the blade with his hands. The ballasting material, which was quarried beside the line, was carried in baskets by large gangs of native girls, who as usual proved able and efficient.

Perhaps on account of the roar of the cataracts there appeared to be few birds in the woods impinging on the river, and so far as I observed, little life of any kind in the neighbourhood of the falls. Every day, however, in going to and from my work I had occasion to pass through a steep cutting in the laterite ; it was only a few yards, but here, protected from the breeze and revelling in the warm sunshine, were literally swarms of butterflies big and little, of sober as well as brilliant colouring, hovering and dancing over *nothing* so far as I could see, but in evident delight in the short life which was theirs. I have frequently mentioned butterflies in these pages, and they have always unconsciously attracted me, but never before had I seen them in such numbers and varieties as here. I could have caught many beautiful specimens, but had not the heart to do so. Clad in beautiful apparel, happy and careless, and entirely outside the cares of this work-a-day world, they almost appeared to me to symbolise the spirit of a people designed by nature to reflect the happy munificence of the sunlit land they dwelt in.

Covering the face of the rocks which bound the river were many ferns and mosses, and amongst others a climbing plant, half fern half moss, which threw out feelers from its fronds and roots, its foliage lying flat upon the surface. Maidenhair ferns were plentiful, and a great number of small flowers hid among the broken rocks which lay scattered through the jungle. Bamboo was as usual plentiful, and in the thicker wood I saw lemurs and peacocks and occasionally a bird of paradise. The jungle in parts was very dense and it was difficult at times to reach the river-side, and in order to obtain one of my subjects here I was obliged to cut a path for several hundred yards before I could reach my point of view. The result, however, amply repaid the labour, as it proved to be quite the finest of a series of splendid views.

Here a number of falls, higher than any of the others, fell into a semicircular basin in which a perpetual rainbow shone, and then shooting half transparent over a sloping ledge of rock, joined waters with the green pool which is seen in the middle distance of the picture I reproduce. The colour of the water was curious, evidently dyed green by vegetable matter, yet perfectly clear, and its range of tint as modified by its varying depths, through which the yellow rock shone, or when broken by cast shadows or reflections, was very beautiful,

A Month on the Lashio Line

though as I soon discovered very difficult to realise pictorially. Whatever the cause might be, here as elsewhere in Burma, I found great difficulty in getting enough colour on to my sheet. Either the intensity of light or some quality of the atmosphere seemed to impoverish the pigment used, and what at the time of application appeared full and juicy and of sufficient depth of tone, too often seemed to vanish as it dried, necessitating partial repainting. All through my time in Burma this proved to be a constant addition to the many impediments which hampered work.

The lesser growths of the jungle in this district were very prolific, creepers particularly abounding as well as many small plants of succulent habit. Every evening as the temperature fell, the air was pervaded by a heavy scent, rather like the smell of hot bread from a baker's oven, but sweeter, which I eventually traced to the fermenting seed-pods of the convolvulus. Whether this was the cause, or only coincidence, I cannot say, but I found that whenever this smell occurred I was more or less subject to attacks of fever, and the scent had a very nauseating effect upon me. As a matter of fact, this district is a very feverish one, and though perfectly safe to visit for a short time, I found that constant working among more or less decaying vegetable matter told seriously upon my health, and I was seldom without some degree of fever which liberal doses of quinine proved powerless to prevent. Probably owing to its elevation and general moisture, forest fires do not appear to occur here, and the consequent accumulation of decaying undergrowth is no doubt the cause.

Orchids are of course numerous, and the little station-house was festooned with them, though they were not in flower at the time of my visit.

Close behind the station was a pretty stretch of the river, falling in gentle rapids of a few feet and studded with woody islets. Here otters abounded, and the inspector of permanent way shot one through the water, so that, stunned, he was able to catch it. It was a fine dog of about 20 lbs., and for a few days was kept in a kennel. At night, however, its own cries, echoed by a number of others which surrounded its cage, became such a nuisance that it had to be liberated.

Though the Man-pwe falls and the gorge at Goekteik are unquestionably the great features of this most interesting railway, the whole of its length is of extreme picturesqueness, in which the scattered native life adds human interest to forest scenery of great richness.

In the occasional clearings the crops, raised on stages above the moist earth, dry in a sun which bleaches the straw to the same whiteness as the weathered tree-trunks. Through forest glades are glimpses of rivulets spanned by quaint native bridges. Along woodland paths, or trudging beside the line, are Shans tattooed round the waist and legs, and in the centre of the chest, carrying on their backs their bedding and such utensils as their basket-work pocket may contain. Others bear bales of merchandise for

A Month on the Lashio Line

some distant market, or in baskets suspended from bamboo poles carry their "household gods," and occasionally their infant children. All are armed with a "dah" hung over the left shoulder by a scarlet cord and tassel, often beautifully made weapons and sheathed between two well-shaped pieces of bamboo or wild plum, bound together with vine tendrils or finely plaited fibre. These are some of the incidents which give variety to the "road," and at the stations the clanging of the piece of railway rail which serves the purpose of a bell, assembles on the platform all the mixed types and nationalities which characterise the Northern Shan States, curious to witness the infrequent arrival and departure of a train.

CHAPTER XII

HAVING accepted an invitation from Mr. Kindersley to pay a visit to the Great Eastern Mines, I left my luxurious car at Hsipaw, and, accompanied by Mr. E. A. Sulman, the mines manager, on the morning of the 12th of February started upon the fatiguing ride over the mountain ranges to the north.

Everything was enveloped in a damp fog as, mounted on rugged little ponies, we left the station and commenced the ascent of the hills over which our road lay. The ground was steeply undulating, and the indaing forest which covered it was practically bare of leaves and offered no protection from the sun, which, fiercely hot, presently poured upon our backs and the dusty road we traversed.

With the exception of the palms and a few evergreens, the forest trees of Burma are deciduous, and particularly in the dry zone and at this period, the green umbrage of spring gives place to sun-bleached boughs and trunks and an undergrowth of parched and withered shrubs.

218

Camping in the Northern Shan States

Lying in and about their roots are drifts of forest debris, which, dry as tinder, crackle under foot as you pass. The trees above are skeletons, and excepting in the deep valleys where subterranean drip preserves some vestige of greenery, the forest might be dead. This is the season of forest fires, which in the economy of nature no doubt serve a useful purpose, but against which the forest officer wages constant war in his efforts to protect the teak and other economic trees from injury. This is done by cutting wide "lanes" through the forests in which they grow as "interceptors" to the farther progress of the flames, and so far as I have learned this precaution is usually efficacious.

In the district through which I was travelling, however, "protected" trees are few, and no European official is here to interfere with the administration of his state by the Sawbwa of Hsipaw, the native prince, and nature is left to the solution of its own problems.

How these fires originate is uncertain. In many cases no doubt they arise through the carelessness of nomadic parties in neglecting to extinguish their camp fires ; but I am told that they are generally spontaneous, and it has been suggested that a probable cause is the rubbing together of the silica-coated bamboo stems as they sway in the breeze.

Whatever their cause may be, and however disastrous their effect, there is no gainsaying the fact that these fires are picturesque to a degree. At night especially they are a beautiful sight, and I have often watched their sinuous lines slowly ascend the sloping hills, alternately bright with flame, or dully red as they burn themselves out. On a still night the roar and crackle of the fire may be heard to a great distance, and the whole effect is weirdly picturesque. By day the fire is less apparent, sunlight enveloping the flames, only the silvery smoke wreathing through the valleys and the blackened track it leaves behind showing the existence of a conflagration.

On this ride to the mines, however, I was to make their nearer acquaintance. In various directions fires were burning, and our track often led through stretches of burnt-out undergrowth and blackened tree-trunks still hot and smouldering.

Unlike the prairie fires of the West, these conflagrations travel slowly and do not engender the same fear for life and property as elsewhere, so that when we suddenly found our farther progress threatened by fires which raged on either side of our path, we only experienced a momentary hesitation before proceeding. As it turned out, however, the fire was of greater extent than we had imagined, and we soon found our narrow track closely hemmed in by jungle now fully alight, and our retreat cut off behind us. Unable to stay where we were, nothing was to be done but push on at our best speed. Fortunately the path was well defined, and as there was no wind it was not crossed by the flames, so that provided we were not headed off in front the danger appeared to be slight. For two hours we rode through flame and smoke, which singed

A MOUNTAIN TORRENT

the hair on our ponies' legs and choked us with its heat. Deer and sine broke from the thickets as the flames caught them, birds wheeled screaming over nests in which their young were being consumed, themselves presently to fall asphyxiated into the flames. Swarms of insects fell from the trees to earth, and what was the fate of the squirrels, snakes, and tree frogs admitted of little doubt.

Presently a serious danger threatened us, as forest trees, burned through at their base, fell crashing into the blazing undergrowth, so adding fresh fuel to the flames which, leaping upward amidst a shower of sparks, soon enveloped their dry crests in a sheet of fire. Had any of these trees fallen across our path the situation would have been serious, but as it was fortune favoured us, and an exciting episode ended happily on our reaching a rivulet which limited the area of devastation, and in whose cool water we were glad to bathe our scorched feet as we lay among the reeds which fringed it.

Viewed afterwards the effect of these fires is often curious. Many trees lying upon the ground were burnt to a white ash but still retained their form until touched, when they crumbled into dust; others of harder texture remained practically intact, except that the softer core had been entirely burnt out, leaving the trunk a fire-hardened cylinder, and it is a common practice among the Burmans to hollow logs in this way for use as water pipes or pumps. Blackened and destitute of life, a burned-out forest is a melancholy sight, but a month or two later rejuvenescence begins, and all signs of desolation are soon lost in the mass of foliage and flowers which spring to life with the same exuberance as before.

The vitality of plants is as extraordinary as their luxuriance, of which I may give an instance. Lying about the ground were many varieties of seeds, among them being one about the size of a nutmeg, hard, and covered with spines, several specimens of which I picked up as curios, but afterwards mislaid. Six months later, after my return to England, I found in the pocket of my kit-bag one of these seeds which showed evidence of sprouting, so, potting it, I kept it in a warm place and carefully tended it. Nearly a year passed without result, but, wishing to experiment further, I repotted it in leaf mould, in doing which I discovered that the seed had separated into three lobes, though the sprout itself was no bigger. Continuing to water it, in August last I was rewarded by the appearance of a small brown shoot above the soil, which a week later had developed into a woody climber, two feet in height, bearing large leaves like a convolvulus, and it is still growing rapidly ! No wonder then that in these forests, where every condition is favourable to growth, vegetation is prolific.

Though in many places there were bad bits, for the greater part of our way a well-made road eased off many of the difficulties of the journey, though the steepness of the hills rendered it tiring for both man and beast. The scenery was very fine, high hills alternating with stretches of flat land, cultivated in patches, and through which ran shady rivulets.

Many spots of extreme beauty recall themselves to my mind. At one place we rested our ponies under a huge banyan-tree, which from one central trunk spread its enormous limbs over an area of close upon an acre. Beneath it was a rest-house where we lunched, and in its deepest shade a little shrine and zeyat for pilgrims. Here also, the ground being open, I was able to measure a cotton-tree, the height of which I found to be 125 feet, though this was small in comparison with many I had noticed in the denser forests.

Another spot I remember with pleasure was the little village of Man-sam. The road being well defined I had ridden ahead of my companions, and eventually reached a point which my pony refused to pass, but, breaking sharply to the right, carried me to the village where I was soon lost among the narrow causeways which wound among its well-stocked gardens. Presently I emerged upon a knoll crowned by an interesting group of kyaungs and pagodas, from which I obtained a magnificent view across immense stretches of hills and forest to distant mountains far away in China. This was quite one of the finest panoramas I had seen, for a view of which I had to thank the obstinacy of my pony ; an obstinacy, however, which proved to be justified, as, on " harking back," I found I should have taken a path which broke off at right angles to the left of the road at the point where we had our disagreement.

High woodlands alternated with deep valleys, green

and cool, in which the creepers were perhaps more fantastic, and the growth of ferns and fungi more prolific than I had seen hitherto. Many of the trees also were strangely formed, growing in curious elbows and abrupt bends difficult to account for, but which gave this portion of the forest a character all its own.

Presently, debouching upon a strip of well-cultivated lowland, we reached Ta-ti, a village built upon the banks of the Nan-tu river, which, rising somewhere in China, eventually joins waters with the Myit-ngé at Hsipaw. Here we rested in a little tai while tiffin was prepared in a cooking-hut adjoining. The scene was very pretty. Emerging in a broad sweep from between mountains which reach altitudes of 6000 and 7000 feet,[1] the river, here 150 yards wide, ran swiftly between wooded banks, its sparkling blue telling strongly among the sunlit foliage. Natives passed to and fro in dug-outs or were engaged in fishing at the head of the rapids below. Women came and went, some to bathe, others to fetch water in buckets made out of a section of bamboo, and at the water's edge "dobies" plied their trade. Around us grouped the head men of the village, kindly souls solicitous for our comfort, and on the shelving bank at our feet, the pack-mules relieved of their burdens, rolled in the dust. These pack-mules are sorry-looking beasts, small and shaggy, but hardy and sure-footed, and they will carry their loads of 140 lbs. for long distances and over any kind of ground.

Here we had to cross the river, and collecting their

[1] The highest point in this district is, I believe, 7579 feet above sea-level.

scattered pack by a shrill call rather like that of a peacock, our Shan drivers swam the mules and ponies across, ourselves and baggage being ferried over in canoes, then, loading up, we restarted on our ride.

The method of loading pack animals is interesting. The baggage, usually carried in boxes or "pahs," [1] or wrapped in canvas coverings, is tightly lashed on to "cradles" of wood shaped like an inverted V, which when loaded are lifted bodily and placed across a wooden saddle firmly girthed over a pad of cloth or fibre. The lashings consist of leather thongs many yards in length, and the natives are good packers, and have a wonderful knack of equalising weights so that a balance is obtained. They have a curious craze, however, for excessively tight binding, and I often feared for the safety of many "breakables" in my pahs, and almost invariably was obliged to ease off the thongs considerably.

This method of loading has many advantages. The centre of gravity is low, and the pack being loose is easily lifted off when halted; and, as often happens in a "jam," or after collision with rocks or tree-trunks, the load tumbles off the back of any fallen animal and it is able to regain its feet unassisted.

I will not enlarge upon the scenery, which differed little in essentials from what I have already described. The rarity of animal life, however, was marked. I saw few birds, and even insect life was not particularly noticeable, and nowhere could I see traces of big game. Once or twice we were followed overhead by troops of

[1] Two baskets of matting—one fitting over the other as a cover.

monkeys, large brown fellows with long tails, who chattered and screamed at us from the boughs, and here also I saw a new variety of snake, which I have not been able to identify. We were riding through a cutting in the sand when I noticed the snake descending a smooth and almost perpendicular tree-trunk, with its body perfectly straight, and without any visible undulations. It wriggled slightly in crossing the path in front of me, but again skimmed up the surface of the steep cutting, apparently without any lateral motion. The snake was a pretty one, and I should think about four feet or more in length ; slender and coloured brown, with longitudinal stripes of green, in which were spots of red at intervals of a few inches. From the shape of the head I judged it to be harmless, but as it instantly disappeared among the undergrowth I had no opportunity of examining it more closely.

I need not describe our camp at Pang-long, where, pitched on a pleasant greensward, our small " double-fly " tent shared with an ancient pagoda the shade of a group of spreading mango-trees. Our next halt, however, furnished an episode. This was at a Chinese settlement called Myoung-young, which boasted a rather large bazaar. In riding through it our attention was caught by the familiar red label of "Bass's Pale Ale," stuck over a shop door. Hot and thirsty, we determined to investigate, and dismounting, Sulman interrogated the proprietor. Burmese and Hindustani being alike foreign to him, Sulman pointed to the label, saying, " John, have you got any of *that* ? " With a beautiful smile " John " in turn pointed to a shelf on which reposed, cobwebby and dusty, four quart bottles. We each secured a bottle, at the price of Rs.2 a-piece, and returning to camp, knocked the heads off the bottles, and enjoyed the unaccustomed luxury of a glass of beer as we had never in our lives done before !

Our road had been generally parallel to the river but separated from it by a range of high hills. On the evening of the second day a sharp turn and steep descent brought us to the river at a point called " The Rapids," where the headquarters of the mine had been established. In response to Sulman's revolver shots we were soon put across by a rope ferry, and a final climb up a steep hill brought us to our destination, the still incompleted bungalow which combined office and home for Sulman, and Park, the mines engineer.

The distance we had covered in the two days was only forty miles, but I confess to having been more completely done up by this ride than either the mileage or the nature of the ground would seem to justify. The following morning and for some days after, fever had me for its own, and for the first time I was unable to work, but lay stretched upon a cane chair enjoying the view from the bungalow, and also Barrie's delightful *Little White Bird*, which with great luck I discovered in a packing-box among a lot of waste paper.

The immediate neighbourhood of " The Rapids " was interesting. Below ran the Nan-tu, impetuous and broken, and here joined by the Sterne river, a mountain stream which rose not far above the mines

Burma

I had come to see. On the shingle bed below, and stretching some distance up the valley, was the mining camp, or, more correctly speaking, village of bamboo huts, its heterogeneous population being engaged in felling timber in the forest, or constructing the railway line by which the mines themselves were eventually to be reached.

A year before this had been an uninhabited waste, which even the birds and monkeys seemed to shun. Now the population of the village was, roughly, 1000, composed of Indian coolies, Shans, Kachins, Yunnanese Chinese, and Burmans, all perhaps bad specimens of their race, but here apparently living on good terms with each other, and all submitting to the quiet domination of two young Englishmen. Indeed, I was strongly impressed by the combination of pluck and good-humour with which Messrs. Sulman and Park maintained discipline, and exacted honest work from this motley crowd of more or less lawless men and women, over whom they had no legal authority, and with whom, in many cases, they had not even a language in common.

It was a position demanding the greatest self-control and courage, and by no means unattended by risk. Let me give a specific instance. The Chinese New Year's Day had just been celebrated with the usual firing of guns, letting off fireworks, and festivities generally, and as a concession to the occasion, the inevitable gambling-house had been allowed an extension of time from 10 to 11 P.M. The day following

ENTRANCE TO THE KUTHODAU. MANDALAY. *See pp.* 250-253

the festival my hosts found the gambling-room again open far beyond the ordinary hour of closing. Without a moment's hesitation, single-handed and only carrying riding-whips, they raided the place, confiscating both money and appliances, and clearing it of its half-drunken and fully armed habitués. Needless to say, their lives were absolutely at the mercy of the crowd, to whom the adjacent Chinese frontier offered an easy asylum ; but "grit" and personal force of character accomplished more than many a fully armed party would have risked.

This was one of those incidents which make for pride of race, and I have among my curios the little antique Chinese saucer used for collecting the "pice" of the gamblers, which was among the spoils that night, and which I treasure as a memento of the episode.

A few days later the house was allowed to open as usual, and on the only occasion on which I visited it it was a wildly picturesque sight, though the crowd was for the most part orderly, and entirely respectful to ourselves.

Among the mixed nationalities here the Chinaman steadily gained in my estimation. All the servants in the bungalow were Chinese, and I found that the liking for them I had previously formed increased upon further acquaintance. They are excellent house servants, and as skilled mechanics are far above their Indian neighbours. I could not help noticing the difference between the work of two carpenters employed in putting up the balustrading to the verandah of the bungalow. The one man was an Indian, content if the timbers fitted approximately, and relying upon nails to complete the job. The other, a Chinaman, would have nothing but a perfect joint, shaving and paring till the part fitted with perfect accuracy, and in many other ways I noticed the same care expended upon whatever work they had in hand.

Among other people with whom I came in contact here were the Kachins, many of whom had come into camp. I had no opportunity of learning much about their habits and customs, but their costumes interested me and perhaps merit description. Most were clad in a heavy woollen jacket and short wide trousers of dark blue with insertions of red, the women adding a short skirt of the same colours and material, prettily fringed and embroidered, and hooped with rings of white bamboo, much like a crinoline, only in this case the hoops are *outside* the skirt. Their hair is tied in a knot upon the top of the head, much like the Burmese, and bound round by a narrow scarf of some thin material, always brightly and variously coloured. In some cases the hair is allowed to fall over the face to the level of the eyebrows, the women covering theirs by a coloured cloth folded flat upon the head. The ears are bored, but instead of ear-rings, are often pierced by a large cigar, or a curious silver ornament about five inches long, shaped like a candle-snuffer, and from the wide end of which falls a scarlet tassel. In most cases hanging under the left arm a prettily embroidered bag serves as a pocket ; and though none of those I saw were armed, I am told that they use bows or cross-bows, and flat-headed spears, the shafts of which are ornamented by coloured cloth and tassels. Altogether they are a quaint people, strongly Mongolian in type, though occasionally good-looking.

The thirteen-mile ride up the Sterne valley to the mines was peculiarly interesting. The rushing little stream winds through a tortuous and rather precipitous valley, its waters coloured by oxide of iron, lead sulphates, and carbonates of copper to a curious opalescent tint, which contrasts prettily with the purer green of the Nan-tu, into which it flows.

The steep hill-sides are densely covered. Trees of all kinds, including rubber, rise in tiers from the water, all more or less smothered in creepers, glorious among which is the purple wisteria, whose flower cones, instead of hanging pendent, stand up above its foliage like the lupin. Large clumps of wild bananas give variety to the stronger greens, among which are splashes of scarlet flower and the delicate drooping leaves of the areca palm. Drooping chains of flowering convolvulus connect this mass of vegetation with the giant grasses, which, often twelve to fourteen feet in height, spring from among the fawn-coloured rocks which form the river bed. Alternating with the trees are forests of bamboo of many varieties, male and female, each species growing separately in large masses without inter-mingling with the others or losing its own individual character. Ferns of many kinds abound, covering the dripping rocks with greenery, and among other varieties

Burma

was a *climbing* fern which half hid the lower tree-trunks to the height of twenty feet. The whole valley was a garden of loveliness, in which seemed to be summed up the vegetable glories of the country. Nothing could exceed the beauty of it all, viewed as it was under the varying effects of mist and sunshine, tropical downpour and the mellow tenderness of twilight! Yet it was a deadly district; fever lurked in every mist, and the smell of decaying vegetable matter or fermenting seed-pods nauseated me.

The interest of the ride, however, kept me going, as we alternately zigzagged across the rough river-bed, scrambled through the steep cane brakes, or made our precarious way along rocky ledges, whose height often made me dizzy.

In contrast with the lower valley, the hills immediately around the mines were devoid of timber, all having been cut down long ago for fuel, and our last two or three miles was a hard climb through rough grasses and dwarf tree-ferns over hills of considerable height and excessive steepness. On some of the hills I found ordinary bracken growing in large patches, much as at home, but as we descended into the warmer and more humid valleys it became rapidly larger, until at the water level it had developed into a fern fourteen feet in height, each frond of enormous size, and supported by a stalk black as ebony and thicker than a stout walking-stick. Some idea of their dimensions may be gathered from the fact that we sheltered, mounted, under individual leaves during a heavy thunderstorm which overtook us.

Camping in the Northern Shan States

The mines themselves lay in a gulch which wound among the hills ; for 500 years worked by the Chinese for silver, they have for the past fifty years been deserted, but about the innumerable smelting furnaces which still remain are huge mounds of slag, consisting, I am told, of practically pure lead, which it was the intention of the Great Eastern Mining Company to remove to the Rapids for refining preparatory to export. To this end Park had been engaged in building the light railway which, by way of the valley we had just traversed, was to connect the Rapids with the mines. Not being a mining expert I can offer no opinion as to the value or purity of the lead deposits, or the possibilities of the streaks of copper everywhere showing in the rocks, but I *can* express appreciation of the splendid manner in which the many and great difficulties in the construction of the line were one by one overcome.

These mines are of great extent, and at one time had been famous throughout China, and all along the ridges of the hills which encircle them are still visible the earth-works and redoubts by which successive Emperors thought it worth their while to guard them.

Along the river, spanned by quaint Chinese bridges, are the ruined homes of many generations of miners, whose galleries cut for immense distances through the living rock open yawning from the valley. In one place are a pair of leogryphs and the staircase leading to the platform of a pagoda which has long since disappeared, and in another was discovered a large inscribed bell, the gift of a former Emperor to the famous mines many long years ago. It is a mournful place, however, whose remains savour rather of the skeleton, and have none of those romantic memories which usually cluster round what is old.

Our quarters for the night consisted of a range of low mud huts roofed with corrugated iron, which, however, proved to be quite comfortable, and as the temperature had gone down to 40°, we ate our dinner in the warmth of a bonfire of packing boxes and such scrub as could be found, round which we afterwards sat and talked till bedtime.

As I was still far from well, and in order to avoid the excessively steep hills by which we had come, we decided to return by the river bed.

In spite of a natural love for the horse, I am not a believer in his "great intelligence," and I had frequent cause in Burma to complain of the stupidity of my mount. It is only fair to say, however, that these Burmese ponies are wonderfully clever with their feet, of which my ride back to the Rapids afforded a rather striking proof.

The river was rough and tumbly, full of boulders and small cascades, and quick alternations in depth which the discoloration of the water effectually concealed. It was very difficult riding, as the stones were slippery and the force of the water considerable, yet my pony took it all without a mistake.

After some seven or eight miles of blind stumbling, the valley widened a little and we found a track which we thought would eventually join the railway. The path was narrow, on one side being the stream, on the other the precipitous hill-side, covered with jungle and creepers and practically impenetrable.

A sudden thunderstorm broke over us, quickly changing the mountain stream into a raging torrent, while the rain and mud added considerably to the difficulties of an already uncertain bridle-path. Sulman elected that it "wasn't good enough," and tethering his pony to a tree, left it for one of the men to bring along, he himself returning on foot through the water. I decided to ride on, as the path seemed to be quite a possible one. I found, however, that the already narrow track still further diminished, and at the same time rose higher above the river, so that I eventually found myself in the unpleasant position of being unable to turn, while thirty feet below me was the stream, now in high flood, and above, a mountain-side almost too precipitous to support any growth, and quite impossible for climbing. Indeed, I very much doubt whether I could have dismounted at all ; as it was, in one or two places I had to throw my "off" leg over the saddle and sit sideways with my feet dangling over a precipice, while my pony squeezed himself along the face of the cliff. To my great relief, however, the path presently descended a little and visibly widened, though it was still most dangerous riding on account of the mud and trickling water, which rendered it anything but a secure foothold for a pony. Eventually I struck the new road to the camp, still in course of construction, and thought my troubles at an end; I was rather disconcerted, however, to find myself suddenly confronted by a smooth shoulder of rock, which jutted out from the hill-side and effectually barred my way. A deep crack, at about the level of the path, suggested a solution of the difficulty, as it formed a ledge of about six inches in width, the rock above sloping away somewhat. I dismounted and had a careful look at the place, and deciding that it presented no greater difficulty than one or two places already negotiated, I succeeded in leading my pony round the buttress.

My difficulties were not over, however, for a little farther on I discovered that recent blasting operations had left a gap in the road of about six feet in depth, faced by a slab of perfectly smooth rock. A ladder was there for the use of the men, but of course this did not aid my position with regard to the pony. We could not get down to the river, and the only option appeared to be to retrace our steps over the many nervous miles we had just traversed, or for the pony to make a jump for it on the chance of being able to keep his feet on the broken path below. The pony did neither, but after a considerable time of urging and coaxing, and, I must confess, also a good deal of hard pulling at the reins which I was only just able to hold from my position below, the pony elected that he " would have to come," and performed the prettiest feat I have ever witnessed. Gathering himself together, he allowed his fore-feet to slide over the edge of the rock and shoot down the incline, so that he was in the position of his

PORTICO OF THE QUEEN'S GOLDEN MONASTERY. MANDALAY. *See pp.* 250-253

nose and fore-feet almost touching mine, while his hind-feet rested on the rock six feet above. Then, slowly shuffling his feet along until he could stretch no farther, he slid his hind-quarters down the rock in the same manner as he had previously done, and half an hour later we were in camp.

Looking back on this ride I cannot but regard it as an extraordinary feat for any animal, and one which I should have thought was well-nigh impossible, and going over the ground later I could only wonder that we had got over it safely. It is a ride I never wish to do again, and one I do not think I could have dared had I not been under the influence of fever at the time.

In spite of the most careful nursing on the part of my friends, I was unable to shake off my attack of fever, and with great reluctance I decided that any further efforts to work here were useless, and that my only course was to return to Mandalay.

With great forethought Sulman had sent a native some ten or twelve miles down the stream to survey the river, and, on his reporting "good water" all the way, had a raft constructed to take us so far on our journey, and thus avoid a portion of the fatiguing ride over the hills, for which I was hardly able ; and ponies and pack mules having been sent on to Tapang-taung, we waved our adieux to Park and started upon a voyage which proved to be somewhat adventurous.

The raft was as usual of bamboo, manned by two Shans, who, armed with paddles, one at the bow and the other at the stern, were able to control our movements to some extent.

For a mile or two we drifted slowly down the deep and silent river, here running between lofty hills which screened us from any wind, and seemed to focus the hot sun within the steaming valley. Still, the heat notwithstanding, it was a pleasant feeling as, lying among our baggage, we idly floated over the placid water in which every detail of the landscape was repeated.

Presently our speed gradually increased, and a sharp bend in the river revealed an alarming-looking rapid right ahead. Though the Shans were satisfied that they could navigate it we preferred to land, and, scrambling along the banks, over fern-clad rocks and roots of trees strangely contorted by variations of humidity and heat, we reached the head of the rapid and watched them go by, and, the raft behaving well, and the boatmen evidently having experience, we decided in future to take any others as they came.

I had never before shot a rapid, and would not from choice have elected to do so in so frail a craft as a bamboo raft, yet the very element of danger gave an added feeling of exhilaration to the operation. It was certainly a strange sensation as we gradually gathered way and headed for the rocks and breakers which, being on the lower level, we could hardly yet see.

On approaching a rapid—and there were many of them—our Shans would begin to shout and yell in order to frighten away the water "nats"; then through the transparent water the bottom seemed suddenly to rise below us, as, shooting over a water glide at a speed which the force of gravity rendered greater than the stream itself, we entered the long reach of leaping waves and eddies, among which we were tossed about like driftwood.

I noticed that in almost all cases the boatmen steered the raft directly for the largest impeding rock, the compression of water against its surface being such as to automatically fend us off. In the case of smaller stones which we often touched, the raft was gently held by the bow, while the stern quietly swung round as on a pivot, and we went over the rapids without any jar or damage resulting.

I am quite ready to confess to a feeling of nervousness on the first two or three occasions, but with each succeeding one the excitement grew, and we began to anticipate them with the same pleasure as is experienced in putting a horse at a stiff fence.

Whether the native who had " surveyed " the stream had ever seen the river at all is open to doubt, for practically the whole distance was an alternation of deep pools and rapids of various degrees of viciousness. The climax came when suddenly on a double bend we came into the tow of one which terrified even our boatmen. In this case the bar, instead of being more or less athwart stream, ran at an acute angle, which had the effect of turning the full force of water *sideways* into the right bank of the river, here composed of huge masses of rock, against which the water boiled and foamed in high curling waves which it seemed destruction to enter. In a moment we were caught by the current and sent spinning into the vortex, in which our raft absolutely disappeared. Then, reappearing, its bow shot high out of the water and through the succeeding wave; once it was absolutely on its edge, and it was all we could do to hold on. So reeling and staggering, and barely escaping collision with the rocks, we finally emerged from this maelstrom, wet to the neck, but fortunately without loss of life or belongings. This was at mid-day, from which time until nightfall we were obliged to go on without a change, and with the prospect of saturated bedding for the night.

This encounter proved to be the last of the dangerous ones, which was fortunate, as in the buffeting our raft had received many of the bamboos had split, and we were practically waterlogged. Indeed, by the time we had reached our destination the raft was barely above water at all.

At Leone we picked up our ponies, and after a steep climb of 1500 feet up a rough kind of staircase cut in the rocks, we entered the forest, and at sunset started by an unknown track to find our way to Myoung-young, where we intended to spend the night. Quite dark, and with nothing to guide us, it was marvellous that we did not lose our way, but guided by some instinct we managed to keep our direction, and, by dint of hard riding, at 8 P.M. we entered the little settlement, and at last were able to dry ourselves and our belongings at the huge fires which were soon ablaze.

Camping in the Northern Shan States

That night I was very ill, and next morning *crawled* rather than rode to Ta-ti. Here I got rapidly worse, and by evening my temperature was 104° and my heart "all to bits," so that I dared not take phenacetin. However, by constant sponging with cold water and frequent doses of brandy, Sulman pulled me through, though he afterwards told me he never expected me to live through the night, and was mentally debating whether he could have me embalmed, or would be compelled to bury me there! Next day we got safely to Hsipaw, where Dr. Leeds of the American Baptist Mission kindly took charge of me, and by the time I had reached Mandalay a day or two later, I was quite myself again.

So ended my sojourn in the Northern Shan States, during the whole of which time I was more or less ill. Yet, curious as it may seem, and in spite of many incidental drawbacks, of all the scenes of marvellous beauty with which from time to time I had been surrounded, and the interesting and pleasant episodes which had marked my tour in Burma, none recur to my mind with such persistence, or engender such a longing to return, as do my solitary journey on the Lashio line and this brief sojourn in the Nan-tu valley, the fascinations of which were in both cases such as far to outweigh all other considerations.

CHAPTER XIII

THE BURMAN

In the foregoing pages I have endeavoured to convey an impression of some of the principal points of interest characteristic of a country more than usually rich in beauty of many kinds.

I find it impossible, however, within the space at my disposal adequately to describe even a portion of the special features which appealed to me during my tour of the country. Undoubtedly the most pronounced impression I received, and one forced upon me repeatedly while off the beaten track, is the amazing prodigality of nature.

The country literally teems with vegetation, and practically anything will grow there; and, as I have previously pointed out, it is this over-exuberance of growth which has resulted in the elimination from the landscape of whatever of rugged character the country possesses, presenting in its stead that generally placid beauty we have noticed.

Living amidst such environment and enjoying a climate which, to say the least, does not predispose to

The Burman

exertion, one need hardly expect to find a great deal of backbone or moral fibre among the people. Provided by nature with most of their requirements, or at least with the minimum of exertion on their part, the spur of necessity is absent and good-natured self-content results.

Naturally perhaps their thoughts are directed largely to amusement and personal adornment, and one is forced to the conclusion that there is something peculiarly fitting in the adoption of the peacock as their national emblem by a people who modestly entitle the king's throne at Mandalay "the centre of the universe." Conceit and good-nature are perhaps their two most striking characteristics. For many years after the deposition of Thebaw, it was difficult to persuade the most intelligent Burman that any power had been able to overcome the prowess of his country and remove the king from his high position. The majority seemed to believe that Thebaw would reappear one day to resume control of affairs now temporarily administered by white " thakins."

One cannot but regret the introduction of our strenuous Western life into this Arcadia, and, as it appears to me, our occupation at Burma has practically destroyed a nation. Even after Thebaw's deposition the Burmese fought long and ably, but with the final subjugation of Upper Burma the native went to the wall. Placidly accepting the position, he seems to be quite content that we should administer the country so long as he is left in full enjoyment of his gay clothing and sporting events. Meanwhile other races, notably Chinese, Japanese, and Indian merchants, have taken advantage of the new order of things and profited by the increased trade consequent upon a more stable government. The result has been the gradual ousting of the male Burman from all employment, while his own easy-going nature limits enterprise on his part.[1]

The women, on the other hand, have great business capabilities, and conduct most of the internal trade of the country. Despising the indolence of the men, it has become an ever-increasing habit with them to mate with the more energetic males of other countries, and there is springing up a new race in which Burmese characteristics are fast disappearing. An example of the independence of women in Burma was afforded during a trial in the High Court of Rangoon. A woman giving evidence was asked by the judge what she did. "Me keep stall in bazaar." "But where is your husband?" "He stayed t'ome and minded the children."

Personal adornment, though a weakness, is happy in its results, for the Burmese crowd is perhaps the gayest in the world; and it is worth notice that the fabrics they wear are good, and, though the women are often over-bedecked with jewellery, they always wear good stones, paste and imitations being unknown among them.

Like their clothing, many idioms of the language are extremely poetic. Take, for example, the Burmese

[1] The present political unrest, and the late abortive rebellion, would seem to indicate some revival of the national spirit, but upon this I can offer no opinion.

BEAUTY AND THE BEAST

The Burman

ideas of time! The times of day are thus described : "One crow of cock," "Two crows of cock," "Three crows of cock," "Dawn great force," "When the sun is one palm-tree high," "The hour when the hpungyis beg" (9 A.M.), etc. The evening hours are no less picturesque, as for instance, "The time when children lay down their heads," "The time when old men lay down their heads," "The time when feet become silent," "The time when young men go courting" (8 to 9 P.M.), "The return of the young lads" (10 P.M.), when, I am told, begins the courting proper!

Similarly, the names they give their daughters are generally pretty. For instance : Ma Sein (Miss Diamond), Ma San-hla (Miss Pretty Hair), Ma Pan-byu (Miss White Flower), Ma Ma-gale (Miss Little Mother), etc., etc. ; while periods of time are denoted by such terms as "A betel chew," "A pot boil," or "The passing of a train."

Though not essentially a brave race, the Burman has plenty of moral courage of a sort, and apparently an indifference to pain, whether in himself or others. This story will illustrate this attitude. Two Burmans attending a pwe, instead of confining themselves to their native "toddy," procured a bottle of gin and became very drunk. With the valour of liquor upon them, they vowed to "go for" the first thing they met on the road. This happened to be a pi dog, which eluded them in the dark. "Never mind," they said, "we will take the next." The next happened to be an old woman, whom they promptly cut to bits with their dahs. On being accused they replied, "Oh yes, we did it, we said we would, so we had to," and with the most complete unconcern they submitted to the beheading which followed. A Burman will go to execution without flinching, but will often run away and leave his wife and children unprotected if attacked. Dacoits also, though occasionally showing extreme bravery, are much the same, and it is usually a question of which will run first should serious resistance be offered.

Thanks to a very complete and vigilant police system, dacoity seems to be on the wane in Burma, though naturally isolated cases of robbery and violence occur here as in other countries. Considerable ingenuity is often applied to the conduct of a theft, an amusing instance of which came under my notice at Pyinmana. Several men armed with long poles, at the ends of which were tied the prickly leaves of the cactus, lined up alongside the railway and awaited the arrival of the train from Mandalay. As the train passed all shouted, the consequence being that every one in the train put out their head to see what was the matter, whereupon the thieves quickly hooked off all the silk turbans with their "fishing rods"! Shrieks of laughter from the thieves greeted the speechless indignation of the sufferers, who, with many a scratched face, were carried helplessly away in the disappearing train. Bribery also is not unknown in Burma, and I was rather tickled on one occasion in the forest when, replying to a facetious remark on my part, a native looked up and said, "If master will take I will offer."

Like their prototypes in Ireland the Burmans are fond of sport in all its branches, no business being of sufficient importance to interfere with a cock fight or a pony race, and relatively large sums are wagered on these events. So keen are they that in their bullock-gharry races partisans will mow down the grass and remove stones and other obstructions which may possibly come in the way of the wheels of the gharry they are supporting, and from infants to old men all display the wildest excitement during the progress of such events.

This predilection for sport was rather well exemplified some time ago at Pegu. The bund broke, letting in the river which inundated the whole surrounding district, only the roofs of the houses appearing above water. Cattle were swimming about and finding refuge on any eminence available, poultry and other farm stock scrambling up the roofs or drowning in the stream. One Burman, whose house was flooded and his wife, dry but disconsolate, seated on the roof, concerned himself little about wife or struggling live stock, but considering this a heaven-sent opportunity, was seen vigorously paddling about in a canoe, training for a coming race !

Cleanly and simple in their habits, the Burmans live almost entirely upon rice, drinking little else but water, though they chew an enormous quantity of betel nut, which is a good stomachic, but has the effect of blackening the teeth and imparting a curious vermilion tint to lips and tongue. From one day old infants are fed on rice, a small bowl of this and another of water being measured out for them at meals, the amount of each increasing as the child grows. The rice, however, is not cooked dry as in India, but the water being left with it it is soft and glutinous, and is first chewed up by the women before being given to the infant, together with a few drops of water with which to wash it down.

Forbidden by their religion to take life, meat seldom forms part of their diet, and to such an extreme is this principle carried that they sometimes even decline to milk their cows, who become dry in consequence. Fish, however, is constantly used, and in the bazaars, where meat is offered for sale by Indians and people of other religions, the Burmans do not scruple to buy and consume it.

There appears to be no division of class in Burma. In the king's time any one might become a prince, and the office of prime minister or any other high position be attained by people of the lowest rank.

Theoretically all are equal, the holding of office alone marking a social grade. A good instance of this was given me by the captain of one of my steamers, who on one occasion, long ago, had been invited by the Lord High Admiral of the Burmese fleet to attend the ceremony of his daughter's " ear-boring," when a large company had assembled to drink warm lemonade and smoke Burmese cheroots as from the Admiral's box they witnessed the pwe which followed. It was altogether a great festival, and attended by all the ceremony and pomp due to the position of his host, who at that time had power of life or death over every man in the navy. Some weeks later he again saw him, but in the interim he had been degraded, and was now paddling about in a dug-out canoe, cutting and selling kaing grass to the king's elephant-keepers! It was a descent from the palace to the hut, from robes of office to the simple loin-cloth, yet he was the same dignified gentleman he had been before, and though perhaps not so corpulent as of yore, was still smiling and apparently contented with his lot.

The Burmans have few modes of expression in Art. I am not aware of any great literary work having been produced by them, and their music is primitive if pleasing, while—owing, no doubt, to the temporary nature of their homes, due to constantly changing sites—pictorial art is practically non-existent. Such pictures as I have seen are the archaic frescoes on temple walls and vaults, and the distemper paintings used in the embellishment of " tan-yin " or kyaungs. As I have mentioned, these are sometimes good of their kind, and I reproduce two which were painted for me by Saya-Myo, probably the best artist in Mandalay, and which may be taken as excellent examples of pictorial art in Burma.

On the other hand, their silk fabrics are very beautiful, and their silver-work quite the finest in the world.[1]

[1] An authoritative monograph upon this subject has been published by Mr. H. L. Tilly, Collector of Customs, Rangoon.

Burma

This art, however, is only practised in a few centres, such as Rangoon, Mandalay, and Thayetmyo, and is characterised by the exquisite modelling and extraordinarily high relief of the figures or foliage with which they embellish bowls and vases in themselves beautiful in form.

It is in their religious buildings, however, that we recognise the chief expression of their art sense, where, influenced by their environment and imitating the exuberance of nature, they are elaborate in design and lavish in their decoration. Their plaster-work is excellent, and teak carving almost unique. They are fond of introducing human and animal forms into their carvings, from life-sized figures of dancing men and women to the innumerable little effigies of beloos, nats, and other supernatural forms which decorate the eaves and cornices of the kyaungs. In the pagodas, guarded by griffins which have always a highly decorative feeling, a common form I noticed was that of the peacock perched upon a crocodile, no doubt emblematical of the triumph of beauty over what is vile, in which perhaps is also implied a religious parallel.

I remember that on landing at Rangoon a friend remarked to me that I would soon " become sick of pagodas," and certainly the great number one sees on the Irrawaddy and throughout the country generally almost justifies such a remark, every point of vantage apparently being utilised by the Burman upon which to build his temple. It must be acknowledged that they add considerably to the beauty of the landscape, but apart from any pictorial value they may possess, I must say that, far from becoming tired of this continuous succession of temples, I found my interest grow rather than diminish upon fuller acquaintance.

At first sight one temple or pagoda is much like another, and it is a graceful object at that, but on comparing the various periods and styles, what a difference is noticeable! All more or less conform to the graceful "zedi" form of design, yet no two are alike. The plinths are sometimes square, again octagonal or polygonal, receding in successive stages—each differently ornamented—to the base of the dome. This again is built in stages, each representing in conventional form some familiar object, such as the rice bowl, the twisted turban, a plantain bud, etc, until the finial is reached, itself almost always enriched with ornament of individual character, and surmounted by the gilt "ti," which is hardly ever the same in two pagodas. A comparison between the Shwe Dagon in Rangoon, the Shwe-Tsan-Dau at Prome, and the unique bell pagoda at Bhamo will soon demonstrate this. Further, the treatment of the panels, which often lend interest to the plinth, the guardian leogryphs and votive vases, the emblematical tree rising from its architectural base, and the hundred odd architectural and artistic adjuncts which combine in forming any given pagoda are all as distinctive as are the different types of humanity. Moreover, each is beautiful, and far from being "sick of pagodas," my only regret is that I had not sufficient

Burma

time at my disposal more fully to study and analyse the undoubted charm each possesses. When to all this is added the effect of gilding in one case, and the subduing influence of age and weather in another, combined with an infinite variety of environment, the pagoda can never become monotonous, particularly when seen as principal object in a landscape of tropical richness, whose beauties are reflected in one of the noblest rivers in the world, and bathed in an atmosphere which lends an enchantment to the whole.

The number and richness of these pagodas suggest another thought,—that the religion of the Burman is active and living, and though many of these buildings are the tangible expression of the piety of past generations, new pagodas and kyaungs are constantly springing up, while many existing shrines are annually being added to and enriched by devotees of the present day. Indeed, herein lies a danger. In the Shwe Dagon pagoda in Rangoon the religious enthusiasm of the pious has led to structural additions which have seriously impaired the beauty of the building, and the same thing is occurring in other places. It seems to me a pity that such acts of vandalism are not controlled, and I would very much like to see the institution in Burma of a department for the preservation of native monuments such as exists in Egypt,[1] in whose hands would rest the restoration and protection of the best

[1] After I had written this chapter a Bill for the preservation of objects of archæological and artistic interest was announced in the *Gazette of India*, but it could hardly have become effective while I was in the country.

THE ANANDA TEMPLE. PAGAN

The Burman

examples of native art, and whose duty it would be to guide the enthusiasm of present-day devotees into channels of usefulness, and prevent the addition of incongruous excrescences to buildings which are not only historic but architecturally complete.

It is not only in the building of pagodas or kyaungs that the Burman expresses his religious instinct. Every male Burman passes at least a small period of his life as an inmate of a monastery, and the practice of and belief in his faith is universal and evidently sincere; and there can be no doubt, I think, that to the influence of Buddhism is due much that is lovable in the character of the people, as well as the creation of an art at once beautiful and distinctive.

They are affectionate to their offspring, and show unbounded respect to their parents, while the unfettered freedom enjoyed by their women places the Burmese far above the generality of Eastern races. And even if the Burman *is* somewhat indolent and conceited, his indolence is largely that of the gentleman of leisure, while so much of grace and beauty envelops the conceit that we readily forgive it.

All in all, the Burmese are a people infinitely attractive, and when to-day so large a proportion of mankind is given up to ideas altogether material and utilitarian, it is surely something for which to be thankful that in Burma we can still find a country which is a garden of wonderful beauty, and inhabited by a race entirely in harmony with its surroundings, and who understand what is meant by the "joy of living."

Index

Index

Burma

T - #0109 - 270225 - C0 - 234/156/14 - PB - 9780415540988 - Gloss Lamination